100% UNOFFICIAL!

GAMES MASTER
PRESENTS

P9-DNG-944

COOL BUILDS
IN MINECRAFT

SCHOLASTIC INC.

EDITORIAL DIRECTOR
Jon White

EDITOR
Amy Best

WRITERS
Wesley Copeland, Emma Davies, Jamie Frier,
Joel McIver, Dom Reseigh-Lincoln

CONTRIBUTOR
Luke Albigés

LEAD DESIGNER
Adam Markiewicz

DESIGNERS
Andy Downes, Madelene King, Laurie Newman

PRODUCTION
Sarah Bankes, Dan Peel

Copyright © 2018 by Future Publishing Limited
Minecraft © Microsoft Inc. All Rights Reserved.

This product is unofficial and is in no way
sponsored by or endorsed by Minecraft or Mojang.
Distributed by Scholastic, Inc., 557 Broadway, New
York, NY, by arrangement with Future Publishing
Limited. *Publishers since 1920.* SCHOLASTIC and
associated logos are trademarks and/or registered
trademarks of Scholastic Inc.

The publisher does not have any control over and
does not assume responsibility for author or third-
party websites or their content.

No part of this publication may be reproduced,
stored in a retrieval system, or transmitted in any
form or by any means, electronic, mechanical,
photocopying, recording, or otherwise, without
written permission of the publisher. For information
regarding permission, write to Future Publishing
Limited, Richmond House, 33 Richmond Hill,
Bournemouth, BH2 6EZ, UK.

ISBN: 978-1-338-32532-4

10 9 8 7 6 5 4   20 21 22

Printed in the U.S.A.   40
First edition, November 2018

WELCOME TO
COOL BUILDS
IN MINECRAFT

Minecraft is a worldwide sensation, with people all over the globe picking up their controllers and tapping away at their keys to immerse themselves in its vast world. With cubes of different materials and sizes at your disposal, you can make pretty much anything you put your mind to. That is where Cool Builds in Minecraft comes in. We have put together some of the coolest big and mini builds for Minecraft novices and experts to try. From stone statues to towering tree houses, there is sure to be something to challenge you or, at least, add a bit of extra decoration to your Minecraft world. So what are you waiting for? Get building!

Contents

BIG BUILDS

MINI BUILDS

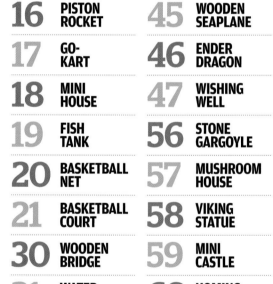

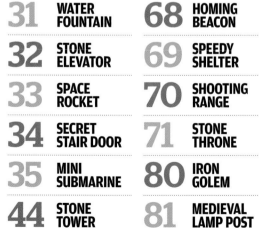

BUILD A HOT-AIR BALLOON

Take a flight of fancy with this steampunk-inspired balloon build.

W

hen it comes to means of transport, nothing seems quite as magical as a hot-air balloon — after all, they're basically harnessing the power of fire. Okay, we'll admit that this creation might not be able to *actually* take you around the world in 80 days, but it certainly looks rather magnificent. We've taken inspiration from Victorian steampunk (basically old-fashioned sci-fi — turns out those guys had quite the imagination!) to design you a build that's fairly straightforward but has *baskets* of style.

01
SET YOUR BASE

Once you've decided where to place your hot-air balloon (we went for the edge of the jungle, so that the balloon starts to rise atmospherically above the trees), you need to start with a platform to work from. It's impossible to build into thin air, after all. Build yourself a platform of 8x8, raised up approximately five blocks from the ground. If you want to go higher or lower, it's totally up to you!

02
BUILD YOUR BASKET

Using spruce planks, lay down a 6x6 square, and then build up around the edges to form walls — giving you a space that is four blocks square. Use more planks to create a roof, giving yourself a room that is three blocks tall. Add in a spruce door on one side and some windows on the others. You could use clear glass for these, but we went for red, orange, and yellow stained glass to add to the Victorian effect.

03
TIME TO DECORATE

While you're in your "basket," you may as well make it look its best. Decorate inside with as much or as little furniture as you like to create a room fit for a Victorian explorer. A large chest for storing items is never a bad idea, and we also went for a row of bookshelves to make ourselves look smart. We added some black and red carpet, plus a picture on the wall. Pretty fancy, no?

04
CREATE A VIEWING DECK

Place three blocks of spruce planks outside your door to act as a porch, then attach a ladder from there up to the top of your basket. Place a block of spruce planks on each corner of the roof, and then fill in the sides using blocks of spruce stairs (with the taller ends facing toward the outside). Make sure you leave a one-block space where your ladder is, for easy access. You've got yourself a viewing deck!

05
RAISE YOUR BANNERS

Time to decorate your deck. Place colored banners on top of the stairs next to each corner (make sure you leave those corner blocks free, as you'll be needing to use them in the next step). Red and orange are good choices here, to keep with the theme we set with our windows, but it's up to you. You can also dot torches around like we have, or even add potted flowers if you fancy a bit of a roof garden!

06
A BIT ROPEY

Now it's time to create the "ropes" that will connect your balloon canopy to the basket you've just finished. Not that we're *actually* going to use rope for this step, mind. On top of each of those blocks of planks we just told you to keep free, place a spruce fence post and then stack two more on top. You should now have four poles, one in each corner, going up three blocks into the air.

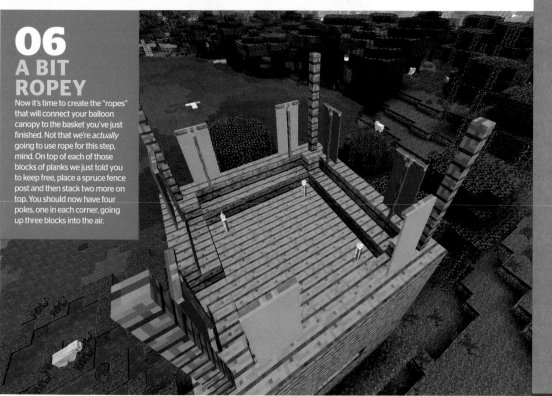

PROPEL YOURSELF

1 You've got to pick your propeller's location, which means imagining in which direction you'd like your balloon to travel. Once you've decided on that, you'll know which side of your basket is the "front" and which is the "back" — we'll be attaching the propeller to the latter. We'd advise making sure that the door is on one of the sides, just to keep things nice and tidy.

2 Using spruce fence posts, build an axle to attach the head of your propeller to. You want to give it enough clearance from your basket to be realistic (nobody wants a basket destroyed by propeller blades) but not to go so far out that the propeller looks unstable. About three blocks outward from the back end of your basket should do the trick.

3 Now you can start work on the head of your propeller. Using blocks of white concrete, first place one block at the base of the axle you made in the previous step. Now position a further four blocks next to this one, so that they form a cross shape. You could use any material of your choice here, but we really liked the sturdy look of the concrete.

4 If you're happy with the size and shape of your propeller, it's time to add some fans. Add another block of spruce fencing to each point of your cross from Step 3, going upward from the top block, downward from the bottom one, and out to the sides from the ones on the left and the right.

5 Finally, it's time to add a last bit of decoration. We went for a simple obsidian block in the middle on the middle of the propeller head, suitably mysterious and cool-looking, we felt, perhaps suggestive of our adventures in lands unknown? You could add whatever you like here, though. Perhaps a Creeper head to show your conquests, or something fancier, like gold or diamond.

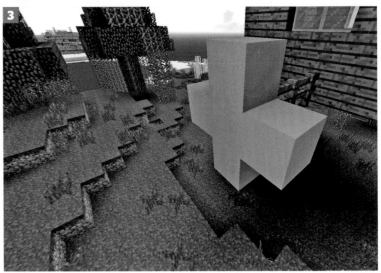

You may be stationary, but no airship is complete without the ability to steer.

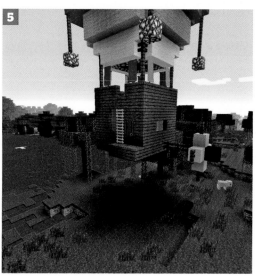

07 CONNECT THE CORNERS

And now to get started on the balloon itself! Using blocks of yellow wool, fill in the gaps in the sides between each of your ropes. Once you've done so, add another layer of yellow wool on top, this time also placing a block on top of your corner ropes. This should give you a 6x6 square of blocks — but don't worry about filling in the whole thing, as you only need an outline that's one block wide.

08 UP AND OUT

Switch to orange wool now, and place a 6x6 square on top of the yellow one you've just built. Now expand this layer outward by one block, so that it measures 8x8 around the outside. Place a second layer of orange blocks over the top — this layer only needs to be one block deep. You'll now see that your canopy is starting to "step" outward. Delete the orange blocks in each corner — this will help the balloon look round.

09
RAISE THE SIDES

Using blocks of red wool, repeat the "up and out" motion you've just completed with the orange blocks. After you've done this twice, build the four sides of the balloon upward by a further five blocks — giving you a rectangle eight blocks wide and six high on each side. Fill in the gap at each corner with a stack of red wool blocks, too. Your canopy will have started to resemble a large bucket at this point.

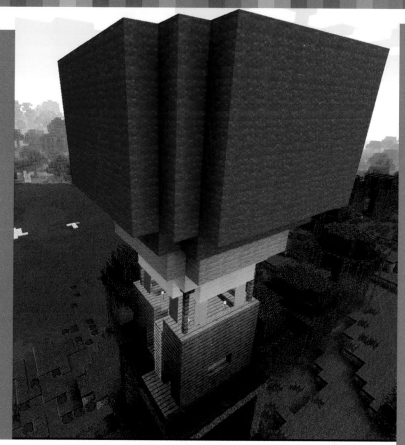

10
TOP IT OUT

In the same way that we went "up and out" before, it's now time to start going up and back in. Add your next layer of red blocks in an 8x8 square on top of your canopy, followed by a 6x6 square of orange that's two blocks tall. Go up and in twice more with yellow wool, and then fill in the middle. Once again, make sure you delete the corner blocks to keep the shape nice and rounded.

13

11 ADD SOME FLOURISHES

Now that your canopy is complete, you can add a bit of extra flair to it. Arrange blocks of yellow and white wool in 4x4 patterned squares on the outside of each side of your canopy — again, this will also improve the shape of the balloon. Add torches to the top and sides of your canopy, too — this will help to highlight your balloon at night, and you may as well make a statement here!

12 GET THE GLOW

To give your balloon that authentic "here be flames" look at nighttime, hop back onto your viewing deck and fill in the hole in the underside of your canopy with glowstone. To keep the feeling of space when standing up here, we added ours in "steps" going upward and inward. That way, we can happily stand in the middle without feeling like our hair is about to be singed off! Yes, we are well aware that won't *really* happen, but we have rather strong imaginations.

13
HANG SOME LANTERNS

To give the final steampunk touch, add spruce fence posts hanging three blocks down from each corner of your canopy. Attach a block of glowstone to the end of each of these "ropes," and you've made some hanging lanterns. Now, all you need to do is delete the initial building platform you made back in the first step, and you've got yourself a masterpiece of steampunk engineering. Whoever said science fiction couldn't become a reality?

LIGHT UP AT NIGHT

If you want a nighttime glow that looks a bit more impressive than torches, why not use redstone lamps? To add these as a decoration, attach two diagonally beside each other to the side of your canopy — perhaps in the middle of the patterned sections you added in Step 11 of the main build. Then, place a daylight sensor on top of one of them (this will power both lamps, as long as their corners are touching). To make sure that your lamps only turn on at night, you'll simply need to invert the sensor — and hey presto! Lamps that automatically light once dusk falls.

MINI BUILDS!

Build amazing things in ten minutes!

BUILD A PISTON ROCKET

1 To begin making this moving contraption, place a sticky piston facing up, then three slime blocks on top.

2 Now add another upward-facing sticky piston and two more slime blocks on top of it. Finally, add a block of redstone to the top.

3 Now destroy the slime blocks above and below the second sticky piston. Next add another sticky piston beneath it, facing down.

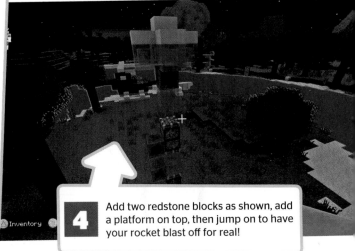

4 Add two redstone blocks as shown, add a platform on top, then jump on to have your rocket blast off for real!

BUILD A GO-KART

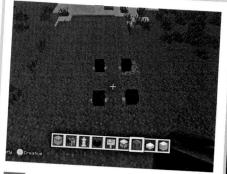

1 To get convincing wheels, dig four holes two blocks deep. Add a slab, then an armor stand and a wither skull to each hole. Place pistons facing inward and redstone to activate them.

2 Add a block over each wheel, place a downward piston then activate it twice with redstone to push the new wheels into the ground.

3 Now that the wheels are in place, and the armor stands hidden, dig one hole in the middle and place a black block for the floor of the kart.

4 Place one stair at the back, then a slab of the same color at the front. Add a sign and an item frame for the steering wheel.

MINI BUILDS

Build amazing things in ten minutes!

BUILD A MINI HOUSE

1 Choose how big the house needs to be (ours is 7x5) and build four pillars linked up by a stone topframe.

2 Now fill three of the sides with your choice of block, and leave space for a window. Fill the fourth wall and leave a smaller space for a door.

3 Now add some glass panes to your Quick Select and use them to fill all the windows. Now add a door (we used an oak door).

4 Create a staggered-looking roof by covering the roof in dark oak wood slabs and dark oak wood stairs.

BUILD A FISH TANK

1 Cut a hole in a wall that's one block deep, four wide, and three high. Now place six vines at the back of the hole.

2 Cut away the middle three blocks, and place two dispensers behind the middle ones and a piece of redstone to the right. Add a fish into each one.

3 Add a redstone repeater underneath the right dispenser, and cover these blocks with ones that match the wall.

4 Place two oak wood blocks at the bottom, two bookshelves in front, two ice blocks on top and a button to the left. Now press the button!

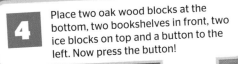

MINI BUILDS

Build amazing things in ten minutes!

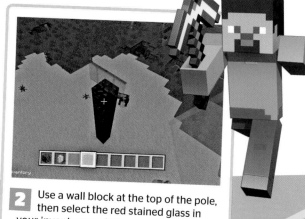

BUILD A BASKETBALL NET

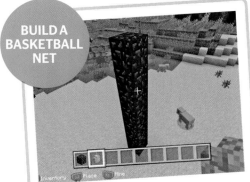

1 First we need a pole, so use any kind of block (we used obsidian) and build it around seven to eight blocks high.

2 Use a wall block at the top of the pole, then select the red stained glass in your inventory and place one on top.

3 Place two panes of white stained glass on either side of the red one, then stack two more white panes on top of these and fill in the gaps.

BUILD THIS!

4 Place a web in front of the wall, then use signs (or a similar block) to build a hoop around the net.

BUILD A BASKETBALL COURT

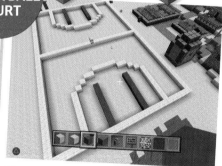

1 For our basketball court, use white wool to build a frame that's 25 blocks wide and 41 blocks long. Add a halfway line in the middle.

2 At each end, count four blocks in and build a line of eight white wool blocks. Then add two single blocks diagonally, then a set of two.

4 Add another ring of blocks around the outside of the first ring. Place a button directly above the redstone dot. Place a water bucket in the dispenser and hit the switch.

3 Add a line of blocks in red hardened clay the same length as the white ones. Add shooting markers then, fill with orange hardened clay.

AUTOMATIC
FARM

Produce massive amounts of
produce with minimal effort.

w ho loves spending time mining up a small amount of wheat, then storing it until they have got enough to make a loaf of bread? No one, that's who. It takes way too long to get enough wheat together for one slice of bread that isn't even as good as a cooked meat. But, what happens if you can have 253 pieces of wheat and around 500 seeds in the time that it takes you to say, "No, wolf, don't jump down that lava-filled hole!"? This guide is all about making the simplest automatic farm imaginable. Plus, there is a windmill, and who doesn't love a good windmill?

FLAT PANELS

Let's start off with an easy one, shall we? Pull out a nice brown dirt block and create a flat 6x7 panel one block above the ground. Head around to the back of the panel, and one block up, on the seven-wide section, build another panel. Then behind the second panel, again one block up, build a third panel so you've got three flat panels, one block up from one another.

THREE MORE
02

Next we'll be adding three more sections. In front of the first panel, lay down a double chest, a gap, a single chest, a gap, and another double. Continue this pattern around to make a square of chests and gaps. Now repeat Step 1, only this time behind the chests. Add in the quartz walls as shown and then mine up your chest guideline. Find the center of the area where the chests were, and place one more chest to mark it.

HOP, HOP, HOPPERS

Crouch down, then add hoppers to all four sides of the chest. This should connect everything together. To test it, try chucking a block into any of the hoppers. If it goes into the chest, you've done it right. Next connect more hoppers coming off the previous hoppers. Above, run a square of hoppers going around the inside of the panels. We'll be mining these ones up in a bit, but keep them there for now so we don't build over.

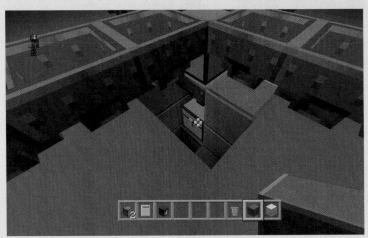

04

CONNECTING DOWN

Remember the rule about crouching down to let you connect hoppers to other hoppers as it'll let items pass through to other hoppers without getting stuck along the way? With that in mind, place a hopper going into another chest below the center chest. Again, try throwing something into the other hoppers and see if it passes through. If it does, replace the center chest in the middle with another hopper and test it out again to be sure it still works.

05

UNDERGROUND TUNNEL

As we're now below ground-level, it's worth making a tunnel leading out. This tunnel will head out from the bottom chest to let us run in and out when we want to collect our crops. You can design this secret entryway however you like, but if you're after a quick design, just replace the walls and flooring with quartz blocks (to match our outer walls) and lob in some sea lanterns in the ceiling so you don't have to worry about any unexpected mobs spawning.

06

REDSTONE AND WATER

Next up, we'll be adding in the mechanism to harvest our crops and begin our redstone circuit. Start by heading to the back of any third panel. Add in a row of wood two blocks in, with sticky pistons below facing upward. Now head around the back and drop in repeaters going into the sticky pistons. Power it up with a redstone torch, then add water behind the wooden blocks. Repeat this on each end of the giant cross.

07

MORE BUILDING

Once you've got your watery dam in place on all four ends, go back to the side with the tunnel leading out. This area will be where our lever goes, but for now, let's build this area up somewhat. It doesn't have to be anything fancy, but as we'll be creating a redstone circuit shortly, we will need some quartz in place to make sure that the circuit doesn't get in the way of the tunnel or vice versa.

08

MORE REDSTONE

Okay. Here's a quick redstone 101 lesson. When you dust a circuit with redstone, the power from the initial lever or torch dulls, meaning the power doesn't travel any longer. To fix this, just add repeaters along the way where the dust dims (facing the way you want the current to travel). As you've probably guessed, we'll now be connecting all the sticky piston repeaters up with dust. Add repeaters as needed and lay a lever by the tunnel.

YE OLDE WINDMILL

Turn back the clock with a different windmill design.

1 This step's all about getting your foundation completely right. Specifically: a giant circle. Start with a row of seven wood blocks (not planks, yet). To the right, place another two one block out, then a diagonal row of three. Now turn, place two more blocks bearing north, then you're safe to run down another row of seven. Repeat this pattern until you have a full circle.

2 Now to build the main tower. With spruce planks, build the base up by an additional five blocks. Next, building from the inside so that it is smaller, build up by seven blocks. Add another section one block in that's five blocks tall. Finish this off by tracing the original circle back up so the top section overhangs the lower sections. Fill in the top area, and the tower is ready.

3 Building a stationary blade that's meant to look like it's spinning isn't easy, but it is most definitely possible. Find the middle of the top section and place two coal blocks coming out. Add oak planks on the four outer sides with spruce fences all the way around in a circle, and add the quartz as shown (ignore the green wool; it's just there so that it's easier to see just what goes where).

4 Minecraft is at its easiest when you break down big sections into shapes. That's what we've done here with the quartz and green wool. Each blade is a two-long strip coming off, a 2x2 square, an L shape, a row of three, another square, and a final two strip. You don't need to use green wool here — use quartz instead — but just like the last step, we've used it to help break this part down.

5 Now all that's left to do is add the outer sections of the blade. Grab your oak wood once more and place it one block away from the main quartz blade. When you reach the three-long section of each blade, stop. Leave the square and two long parts at the ends empty. Then simply fill the gaps with the spruce fencing, and your simple-but-effective windmill blade is complete and ready for some wind.

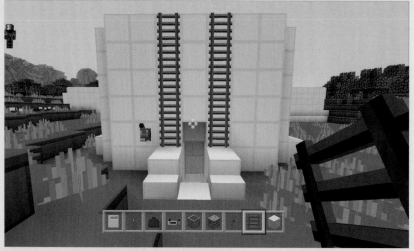

09
COVERING UP

You should be able to build a wall around the tunnel entrance to cover up the redstone at the front (put a repeater on the other side of the block with the lever). Add steps for a simple design, and ladders so you can climb up to replant your crops. You can cover the redstone that's around the outside by building new walls, but to be honest, if you've gone to the trouble of making a redstone circuit, why would you want to hide it? Show it off, we say!

10
REMODELING

Go back to the center of the X. Remove the hoppers level with the dirt and replace them one block lower. This helps as the water will push the crops downward, into the hopper, rather than getting stuck on a flat area. You'll also want to build the quartz area in the center up by a few blocks. This, too, will help with pushing the crops down into the hoppers, as it'll act as a dam.

11
TEST RUN

Are you ready? It's the moment of truth! Plant your crops. We went with wheat, but any plantable crop works. Dust them with bone meal to speed up the growing process, then turn autosave off (to avoid needing to reset everything if it doesn't work). Now go and pull the lever. The wood blocks should fall, and the water will wash your crops down. Pull the lever again to stop the water flow, then head into the tunnel. If it worked, feel free to reload. If not, check that your redstone's all hooked up right.

12

WINDMILL PT. 1

Fill in the area in the center so it's nice and flat. Draw a 5x5 flat panel in the middle and chop the corners off. Build up inside the square by five blocks, then add three blocks in the center of each side of the outside square (to make the T shape). Make a cross shape and build it high, before building a flat shape with two T shapes on the end.

BUILD BONUS

ULTIMATE WHEAT FARM

Apparently, there's a world record for the biggest wheat farm. But how much wheat would one need to claim such a prize? A whopping 90,717 wheat (and up to 272,151 seeds!) is the answer. That's a lot of wheat! Think of how much bread that could make?!

This build isn't just a seemingly endless world of wheat, though. The person behind the build, Alvtron, also went about creating different structures around the farm, including a kitted-out bedroom. They also note that while there is a build that produces around 10,000 more wheat, the sheer scale of Alvtron's build makes it without question the largest wheat farm ever conceived!

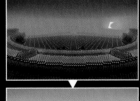

13

WINDMILL PT. 2

Go ahead and build the head of the turbine. This is just a big cuboid built backward with the corners chopped off to create a step effect. Next build seven squares coming from the right of the front T shape with a single block on the last square. Do the same in reverse, only on the left of the T shape, and finish by creating a final, three-wide column going up at three different lengths.

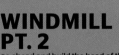

29

MINI BUILDS!

Build amazing things in ten minutes!

BUILD A WOODEN BRIDGE

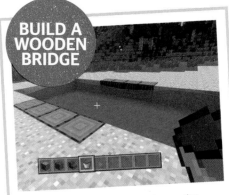

1 We need to dig four holes on the edge of the water and fill them with oak blocks from your inventory.

2 Now add one more oak block on top of the outer two, and one layer of spruce wood stairs in between them.

3 Build another column of three oak blocks in the water in front of the ones you just added. Now add three layers of spruce wood between them.

4 On top of these layers, add spruce wood stairs on the outer two, then two more in the middle, upside down.

BUILD A FOUNTAIN

1 Dig a hole that's two blocks deep and 3x3 in width and length. At the bottom of the hole, make an L shape that's 3x1 in size.

2 Place two more as shown above. Place a redstone on the right block, create a trail around the L shape, then a redstone torch in front of the first block.

BUILD THIS!

3 Next, add a stone brick block on top of the redstone torch, then a dispenser on top. Now place a ring of stone brick blocks around the torch.

4 Add another ring of blocks around the outside of the first ring. Place a button directly above the redstone dot. Place a water bucket in the dispenser and hit the switch.

ive △ Inventory

MINI BUILDS

Build amazing things in ten minutes!

1 Dig a trench four blocks long and three deep. Place a redstone repeater two blocks in and place a building block on either side. Now place a sticky piston on top and place some redstone in front of it.

2 Place a slime block on the piston, then place a heavy block on either side. Now place a heavy block on three of these and set down a button on the fourth. Place flooring blocks around it.

3 Now place a redstone torch on the side of the lowest block in the remaining hole. Place a building block over it and add another torch on this one. Now add four blocks on top of the heavy block.

4 Add a block on the torch, place a torch, then repeat. Place a final block at the top, then a sticky piston. Add another block in front. Now add flooring blocks to make your second floor.

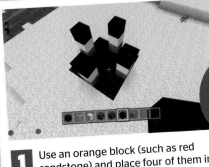

BUILD A SPACE ROCKET

1 Use an orange block (such as red sandstone) and place four of them in a cross pattern (we made ours 4x4). Place an iron block on each one and then a coal or obsidian block.

2 Next, place an iron block to the side of each white block so it's moving inward. Now place another on top. Repeat this for each of the four sides.

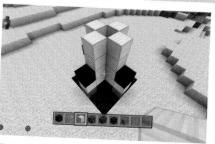

3 Now add an iron block on top of each of the ones you've just placed, as well as the middle. Then place another layer on top of these, but leave a hole in the middle.

4 To finish off our rocket, place glass blocks on top of the iron blocks you've just placed, then add one on its own at the top. On top of this, place a red-colored block (such as red concrete) to complete the look!

33

MINI BUILDS

Build amazing things in ten minutes!

BUILD A SECRET STAIR DOOR

1 Dig a trench that's six blocks deep, eight long, and five wide. In the very center, build four blocks high. Destroy the first and third, place redstone torches as shown, then add three sticky pistons.

2 On the right-hand side, place the blocks and sticky piston down as shown above. Place the repeaters facing to the rear, delaying the first by two. Place redstone behind the front repeater and in front of the second.

3 On the left, place a block at the front and create a staggered step leading to the rear. Place a repeater facing the piston as shown, delaying it by three. Add three torches, and redstone, as shown.

4 Add the foundations beneath, placing three repeaters facing the same direction. Delay the rear one by three and the one in front of it by two.

5 Now add blocks, placing a repeater, torches, and redstone to connect the mechanism. Build a platform around the very top piston. This is a hidden room on which you can then build your stairs.

ASSEMBLE A MINI SUBMARINE

1 Using yellow concrete, build a 4x3 frame. Add another block at the front and lay six glass blocks on top. Now add four yellow blocks at the rear and add ladders on the side and a lever at the front.

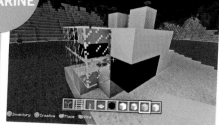

2 To the side of the sub, add two black concrete blocks and two yellow concrete blocks. Add two more yellow ones on top, then add a yellow block on either side of the ladder.

3 Leaving a gap in between the blocks you've just added, place an iron trapdoor on top, then add three glass blocks in front of it. Then add a sea lantern in the middle and two yellow blocks.

4 At the back, add two yellow concrete blocks on the top, left, right, and bottom to create a cross shape. Add black concrete blocks to the end of this cross and a sea lantern in the middle.

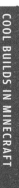

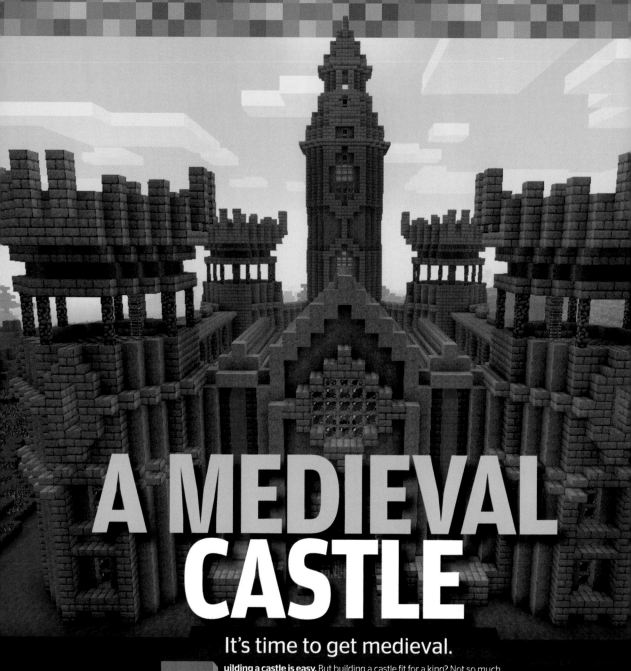

A MEDIEVAL CASTLE

It's time to get medieval.

Building a castle is easy. But building a castle fit for a king? Not so much. How do you build imposing towers? How do you avoid building a boring, flat, one-block-wide wall? How do you even build a throne that looks like a throne?

In this guide we'll show you how to go about creating a gigantic castle minus all the usual hassle that comes with sizing stuff up right. For this build we'll be using the Fantasy texture pack, but as always, don't feel you have to. The Vanilla, Plastic, or City

01
FIRST WALL

Kick-start this monster build by equipping stone and stone bricks. Find a large open area, then build two six-high spikes with a five-block gap in between. Curve the top area together, then build the stone walls on both sides. Make a note of the diagonal block placements on either side and the stone formation in front. Create a circle above the door frame and fill it with glass panes before building the walls below and behind it. Now connect the inner diagonal pillars up and into the window.

02
WALLS AND FOUNTAINS

Knock out a two-wide section in each of the stone walls and fill them with stone bricks one block back. Do this on both sides, then build all the side walls up so they're one block higher than the middle of the window section. Add in the triangular stone sections in line with the stone bricks. Square off the front sections with stone, then add water at the center top of the stone bricks. Don't forget to put a block behind the gap so water only flows on one side.

03
TWO TOWERS

Next up, we'll be adding in some towers at the front. Look to the right side and draw five stone bricks vertically coming from the watery basin. From here, drop two diagonal blocks heading up and right, then place another five blocks horizontally. You should be able to repeat this to complete the circle. Build the tower 20 blocks tall then add in the window sections and the stone brick half slabs as shown.

04
THE SECOND TOWER

Build a second tower, with the same specifications as the first, to the left. Now head to the top and arm yourself with cobblestone walls. Place three walls on the longest sections, and above them, create the circular formation. Now build another circle formation one block in, then above that, another formation in line with the first. Build one final formation one block out and three blocks high, and add the spikes to the side. To finish, just repeat this step on the opposite tower.

05 ENTRANCE WAY

Above the main door frame, build the roof back with stone brick steps. To the left and right, there should be two more triangular sections. Build those back, too. Create from stone, a solid flat wall coming from the under-right side of the roof, with stone bricks on each end. This wall should sit one block under the roof. At the bottom, count two blocks in and smash a 4x3 hole. Count another three blocks, and then do it again. Lastly, poke a hole above each section in the middle.

06 WALL DECORATIONS

Fill the holes with glass panes. With stone brick steps and stone bricks, build the pillar in between the two windows. Run half slabs along the top, add to the pillar again, then add more slabs. Add two smaller windows to the left and right of the upper pillar, then drop in half slabs above and below. Build an identical second wall on the opposite side. For the back section, roughly mirror the front of the castle, but with windows in place of the fountains.

07 MAIN WALLS

Head to the base of the towers, and at the two diagonal sections, build a wall coming from the second block back. For this section, it's best to mimic what we've done in the image to the right. The pillars are slightly modified versions, and when working on the upper wall, remember to build the cobblestone one block back to give it some depth. We went with five sections per wall, but you can adjust this if you want an even larger castle.

08 INSIDE THE WALL

Once you've got a wall on the side of your castle, we need to make the insides look a little less flat. To do this, build around the cobblestone sections with stone bricks so you've got one block of depth on the inside. In between each section, use half slabs for a nifty design. Underneath each of the windows, use stone brick steps to create a support column. Above, on the newly made walkway area, use either wooden fence or stone bricks around the edge.

MORE CUSTOMIZATIONS

With the castle complete, let's now bring it to life.

1 What's the point in a castle without a throne room? To build this lovely luxury, head to the inside of the main tower. Use stone brick steps and slabs for the area around the throne, then build the throne itself from a mix of quartz steps, half slabs, and blocks. Build the floor from cobblestone, dark oak wood, and red carpet. Then just dot some paintings about and it's ready.

2 If we have a throne room, we also need a royal bedroom. Head to the top area of the main tower and lay down flooring a couple of blocks below the windows. The table is just two wooden steps with a half slab, and our chair is just purpur steps. Surround two beds in bricks and slabs, then — just like in the last step — use paintings to round out our look.

3 For the main courtyard area, run chiseled stone bricks along the center to form a pathway. Create an elevated, simple fountain surrounded by steps leading up. Add leaf blocks in the corner sections of the steps to create our hedges. And lastly, use stone to create a path going around everything, before filling in the rest of the floor with gravel.

4 On the opposite side of the courtyard, we're going to build a small market section. This is really easy. Just create a circle (the main length is three), add some fences, then build a roof. Drop villagers in, put an item frame along with an item to indicate what they're selling, then place fences inside the stalls so they can't escape. Simple.

5 This pig has been caught selling counterfeit carrots. Do not speak to him! Behind the front towers, on the inside, is enough space to build a staircase leading down. But what do we put below the castle? A dungeon! Just dig up a corridor, build 4x4 rooms off to the side, spawn an animal, fill the front with iron bars, and that's it!

09 THREE MORE TOWERS

Place down two more circles on the floor, in line with the two front towers. Now build those circles up and create them the same as we did the front towers. For this next part, we'll be building the main tower. Create another circle parallel with the front doorframe, only a few blocks behind the back two towers. This circle's main length is seven blocks. Next, build it up in stages of ten stone bricks followed by five stone. Do this until you have three stone brick sections.

10 DECORATING THE TOWER

Add a door hole at the front, then go ahead and build walls coming from the back two towers into the main tower. On four sides of the tower, build on top of the stone areas to connect each section together. On each of the stone brick panels, knock out holes and fill with glass panes. Make them nice and large so they're visible from a distance. This is our main focal point, after all.

11 TOP OF THE TOWER

This one's nice and simple. Run stone brick steps around the outside of the top of the main tower. All of the steps should curve into one another. If they don't, then just pick them up and replace them. The trick here is to aim each step at the upper-back corner of the previous step. It's a bit tricky to get right, but it's worth it. Afterward, plop down another circle in line with the main tower.

12
MORE WALLS

Okay. That circle you just placed? Build it up by two blocks so it's three blocks tall. Build another circle, only this time one block in. Again, build it up by three. Now add one final circle that is, you guessed it, three blocks high. If you chop off the corners of each wall, that'll help to make it look less blocky. Feel free to throw in some cracked stone bricks, too, if you want a more ruined feel to this tower.

BUILD BONUS

A WHOLE NEW (STEAMPUNK) WORLD

Check this out. Right? Amazing! Our build covers all the basic principles needed to go off and create something as epic as this. Once you understand how to turn circles into towers, how to avoid flat walls and instead create depth-filled sights, and how roofs can be used in all different sizes, the sky's the limit to what you can build. Although this steampunk castle looks complex, once you break it down into smaller sections, taking inspiration and creating something similar doesn't seem all that difficult. Plus there's always the option of roping in a friend to do all the heavy lifting. That's what friends are for!

13
FINAL SECTIONS

For our final step, build another circle one block in, build it up by three, and knock out the north, south, east, and west sides. Run upside-down steps around the top, then create three two-high walls leading inward on each side with a spike on top. Carve out some window areas and fill with glass panes as shown, drop in some cracked stone bricks if you want, and we're done! Feel free to now go off and collapse into a tired heap. You've earned it.

MINI BUILDS

Build amazing things in ten minutes!

BUILD A STONE TOWER

1 Dig a hole that's one block deep and 3x3. Place oak or spruce planks in the floor. Place cobblestone or andesite blocks on either side of the entrance and three on the remaining sides.

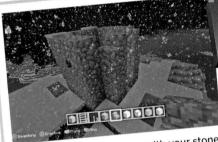

2 Now start building up with your stone of choice. Every two layers, add a cobblestone or andesite stair to create a small window. Repeat until your tower body is as high as you like.

3 Before you start the final section of the build, use those planks to build a central column from the middle of the floor to the top floor of your tower. Now place ladders all the way to the top.

4 Now use a different type of stone block to create a three-block ledge on either side of the tower — including one in the inside corners. Now add a layer on top of this, then alternate blocks and torches.

BUILD A SEAPLANE

1 Start by using a block of your choice — such as a colored quartz — and create two lines of five blocks with a gap of three blocks. Then add stairs in the same color facing outwards.

2 Add six blocks in between the stairs — three in the middle, two at one end, and one at the other — and a slab. At this end, add a black block for the nose and 13 blocks for the body and rudder.

3 Add stairs and slabs to the rudder to finish it off, then use spruce gates for the propellers on the black block. Add carpet at the front, then glass for the cabin. Add more blocks behind it for effect.

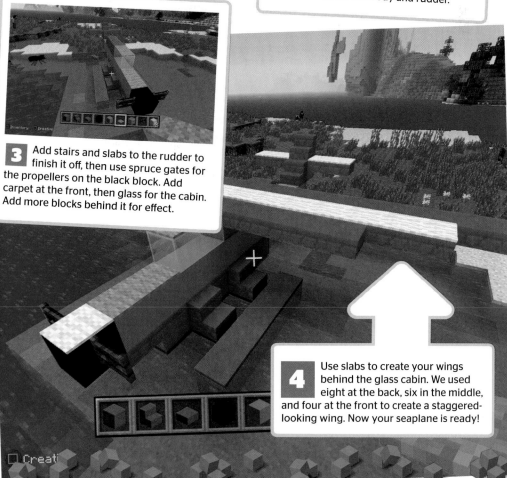

4 Use slabs to create your wings behind the glass cabin. We used eight at the back, six in the middle, and four at the front to create a staggered-looking wing. Now your seaplane is ready!

MINI BUILDS

Build amazing things in ten minutes!

BUILD AN ENDER DRAGON

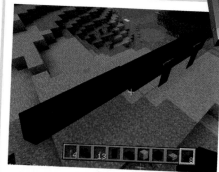

1 For the body and legs, use concrete seven blocks long. Add banners on the sides of the second and fifth blocks.

2 To add and create your dragon's tail, use four nether brick slabs at the rear of your Ender Dragon, then place black carpet over each one.

3 On either side of the third block from the front, place four cobblestone slabs. Add two behind these. Cover each one in black carpet.

4 To finish, add two buttons at the front, three levers, and two buttons. Then add an Ender Dragon head!

BUILD A WISHING WELL

1 Create a 3x3 square of blocks (we used cobblestone), then add a 5x5 square of slabs around its edge.

2 To create the pillars that hold up the well's roof, choose a type of fence, build a pillar of blocks, attach the fences, then destroy the blocks.

BUILD THIS!

3 Choose a lighter layer of slabs (we used oak) that is two slabs all the way around the four pillars. Add water to the well, too.

4 Add a layer of slabs around the gap, then fill this over. On top, place four steps that back onto one another.

HANGING IN SUSPENSE

Build a super-massive suspension bridge with connecting cables.

1

MAKE A ROAD

Drop five coal blocks, a stone block, and five more coal blocks in a row. Extend it toward you to make a road. Every third block in the middle, lay three white wool blocks to make a thin white line.

2

EXTEND THE ROAD

Once you've extended the road to the length you need it, add stone blocks to the left and right sides, and cover the underneath, again in stone blocks. This will stop it looking weird from below.

3

CREATE THE FIRST TOWER'S BASE

Head back to the start, and on the left side add in the quartz block shape (as seen in the image above) to act as the foundation of a tower. The shape is two 2x2 set outside a 4x4 with two rows of three on the top and bottom.

4

BUILD 13 UP

Looking at the foundation, build up the outer walls by 13 blocks, again out of quartz. Don't worry about filling in the middle blocks too much as they won't be noticeable from the outside.

INSPIRATION

TOWER TWEAK Moving the tower sections around can yield different looks.

SIMPLICITY Crafter Ector Vynk shows you don't need elaborate structures.

WRAP AROUND Why not wrap the wire around the bridge, like GoodTimesWithScar did?

5

MAKE SOME STEPS

On the two rows of three, look to the one closest to the road and place a 3x3 section on its face. Add a 2x3 in front of that, then lay another row with some upside-down steps on it.

6

CREATE ANOTHER TOWER

Build a tower opposite the last one. Start from the row of three so it's symmetrical. Build up so it's level, add in the step formation, then connect the two sets of steps with quartz half slabs.

7

BUILD A WALL

Build a wall four blocks high, directly above the steps. Look to the middle, and one block in, build two blocks on top of each other. Continue to the end, and do this again on the opposite side.

8

EXTEND THE TOWERS

In the last step, you built a shaped plate, which looks great from a distance. The only problem now is that your towers are lower than the plate, so build them up so that everything is even.

9

ADD MORE STEPS

Now make it uneven. Create the step formation from below, but the other way: four blocks out, then steps, then three blocks out, and a row of two. Do it on the opposite side. Connect with half slabs.

10

EXTEND FARTHER

Extend the walls so they're seven blocks higher than the step formations. And, once again, build two more step formations — the same way we did the first. Connect with half slabs then move on.

11

ANOTHER SHAPED PLATE

All this repetition will make sense very soon — we promise. For now, let's build another shaped plate directly above the last step formations. As with the last one, be sure to build another shaped plate on the back.

12

THE TOP SECTION

We're almost at the top now. Build another two step formations with walls on the east and west sides that are four blocks higher than the steps. Add two more upside-down step formations above, connect them, and finish by building another shaped plate above.

13

ALMOST THERE

Build the two towers up so they're level. From here, place iron bars across the top of the plate, and build a mini platform one block smaller on top of the towers with a 3x2 spike above. Add steps on to the left and right of the bars, and you're done here.

14

EXTEND AND SIDES

You may have noticed your towers are floating, so let's build the underneath and connect them to ground or sea level. After that, we're going to add flat sections along the sides of the road that poke out by three quartz blocks.

THE SIDES

To create the side sections, build four blocks down from the start and six more blocks out from the bottom. Then with half slabs, place them in a diagonal pattern. When you reach the bottom, add a column, then build slabs in the opposite direction.

15

16

THE SUSPENSION PART 1

This is made of two block platforms in a step formation. The first must be parallel with the lumpy surface of the second shaped plate. Build 23 platforms going down. Lay a straight row of six for the middle. Do this on both sides.

INSPIRATION

STONE BRIDGE As Grian shows, stone blocks can help make a bridge look medieval.

ADD WOOD Using wood also has an old-fashioned feel, like StudMuffinSam's design.

BUILD BIG If you have time, do what BrentGamezz did: Build gigantic castle turrets as towers.

53

17

THE SUSPENSION PART 2

Your two diagonal lines should be parallel. Now build 23 more two-block platforms going up from the row of six. Afterward, grab some cobblestone walls and run them down from every second block.

18

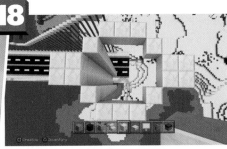

TWO MORE TOWERS

You're almost at the finish line — just two more towers to go. Head to the last two-block platform on the right and build a 2x2 platform behind it. Build the foundation like in Step 3 and extend the whole thing up by 15 blocks and down to ground or sea level.

19

THE LEFT TOWER

Perform the last step again, only on the left. Find the last two-block platform, build a 2x2 behind it, re-create the shape, and build it up by 15 blocks, then down to the ground. Easy as pie (whatever that means!).

20

THE TOPS

At the tops of the two new towers, build one block in and create 2x3 spikes at the top. Run steps around the new sections, and use iron bars in the center, like you did in Step 13.

21

THE SHAPED PLATES RETURN

We're building this section in reverse, so from top to bottom. Underneath the iron-bar section, build another shaped plate. Underneath that plate, drop in two step formations and connect it with — you guessed it — quartz half slabs.

22

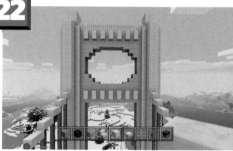

ALMOST THERE

Build two more step formations and a second shaped plate beneath them. Below that, create another circular window by placing four step formations and steps, and connecting them together.

23

THE FINAL STEP

To finish, simply build one more front plate and, below it, two more step formations. If you ever decide to extend your bridge farther, just add more towers and more two-block steps on the sides, and build out the road as far as you need.

MINI
BUILDS

Build amazing things in ten minutes!

BUILD A GARGOYLE

1 Stack two polished andesite blocks. Place two stone stairs upside down on one side, then place two cobblestone walls and stairs on top.

2 On the other side, place two cobblestone stairs facing outward (you might need to add one in the middle to help place them correctly). Drop a slab on top, too.

3 To do this, stack two stone slabs on top of each other, then place stone stairs on either side (upside-down). Destroy the topmost slab to create the head and horns of your gargoyle.

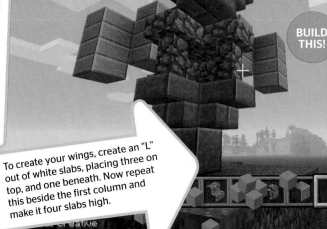

BUILD THIS!

4 To create your wings, create an "L" out of white slabs, placing three on top, and one beneath. Now repeat this beside the first column and make it four slabs high.

BUILD A MUSHROOM HOUSE

1 Use oak planks to create a square 4x5 blocks wide and two high. Leave a gap in the middle for a door, then place blocks outside for roots.

2 To start the roof, use nether wart blocks and quartz and build a square that's 7x6 (make sure it's hanging over your roots below).

BUILD THIS!

3 Add another layer straight up, and make sure you space out the white quartz so it stands out from most of the nether wart.

4 Add another layer one block in from the previous layer, then fill that hole in nether wart blocks. Use bricks to create your chimney.

MINI BUILDS

Build amazing things in ten minutes!

BUILD A VIKING STATUE

1 Place a block. Then use some stairs (we used dark oak) to create a stand around it. Pop an anvil on top.

2 To create your Viking's body, place a cauldron on the anvil, add two blocks on either side of it, then add a second anvil and two hoppers.

3 For a head, use a dropper or a dispenser (as these have faces on the front). Now place a slab (we used cobblestone) on top.

4 Use signs for horns. Destroy the blocks under the hoppers. Use cobblestone walls for hands, and dark oak fence and an anvil for the hammer.

58

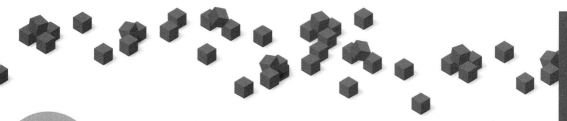

HOW TO BUILD A MINI CASTLE

1 Build a tower that is 3x3, and four blocks high. You then need to leave a gap three blocks up in the middle of each side, and at the top.

2 Repeat this process three more times, making sure that there's a three block gap between each one.

3 Add a spruce door at the front (we used three of them), then use your silverfish stone brick to fill in the walls.

4 Use some stone brick stairs and chiseled stone bricks to add some details to the front and on the top of each tower.

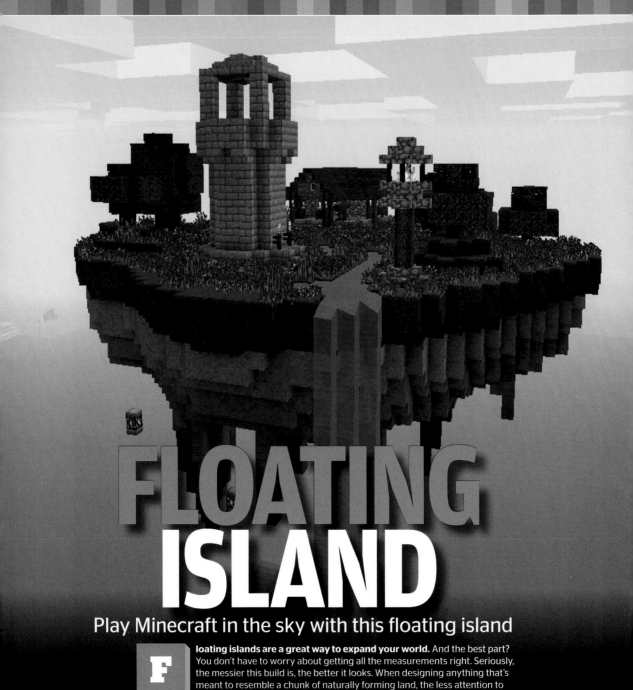

FLOATING ISLAND

Play Minecraft in the sky with this floating island

Floating islands are a great way to expand your world. And the best part? You don't have to worry about getting all the measurements right. Seriously, the messier this build is, the better it looks. When designing anything that's meant to resemble a chunk of naturally forming land, the less attention to detail you pay, the better. I know, right? Crazy . . . In this guide we'll cover how to go about creating your own floating island, as well as how to transform it from a flattened island, into something more realistic. And, yes, we've got some tips for what to build on your island. Aren't we nice?

01
NOT A CIRCLE

Find yourself a large open area above water. You can build it above land, but due to how dark the underside becomes, water is recommended. Next, build a circular shape in the air and fill it in. Just don't make your shape a proper circle. What you're aiming for is a kind of jagged oval shape, as we want this build to look like it has been ripped from the ground. So keep it as messy as possible!

02
THE THICKENING

Now that we've got a flat, floating plate in the sky, we need to thicken it up. Or specifically, thicken it down. Switch from grass blocks to dirt blocks and, directly below the grass blocks, add two more layers below. The reason for the switch to dirt blocks is because we want our floating island to loosely follow how Minecraft spawns blocks: Below grass blocks are dirt blocks, and below dirt blocks are stone blocks, and so on . . .

03 THE NEXT LAYER

Following on from the last step and the idea of basing our island loosely on how blocks spawn, swap out your dirt blocks for stone. Look to the longest side, and below it and one block back, add a row of stone. Follow this all the way around until you have a one-high row that is going around the inside. Now you need to build it downward so it's three blocks in height.

04 TWO MORE LAYERS

Just as we did with the last step, build another layer one block in from the last, only this time make it just two blocks in height. After that's completed, create one last layer, one block in again, that's only one block in height. At this point you may notice everything looks a little flat and solid. Don't worry, later on we'll be going back in and fixing everything up so it looks more natural.

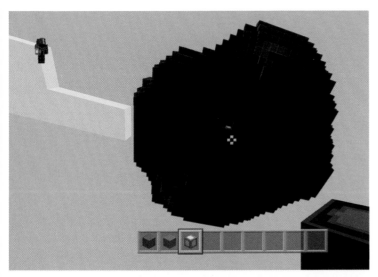

05
STARTING THE SPIKE

Fly on down to the underside of the island. If you want to drop down some sea lanterns for light, go right ahead. It is pretty dark, after all! Once you've got enough light (or popped a night-vision potion), draw a bendy line from stone going through the center. Just as we didn't make our original circle a proper circle, don't make this a straight line or a perfect semicircle. Keep it messy, and when you're happy with it, fill it in so it's flat.

06
THE FIRST SPIKE

These next sections are all about adding some rock formations (called stalactites) coming from the bottom of the island. To do this, in the rough center of the stone section from the last step, build a line going straight down. Now add more lines on each of the sides that are not as long as the first line. Repeat this until you've reached a thickness you're happy with. Just keep in mind the first spike needs to be the biggest.

07 MORE SPIKES

Next we'll be repeating the last step, only on a smaller scale. Fill in the rest of the underneath with stone so it's completely flat. Now add lots of smaller lines coming from the bottom, and again, keep thickening them until you're happy with how they look. Feel free to play around with the smaller ones. Adding random stone shapes onto them is a great way to make them look different from our main spike.

08 ONE QUICK THING

Okay. So this is a nice and simple one. Go directly below the island and look straight up. What we'll be doing here is running a row of stone around the underside to link up all the different spikes. Take a look at the image. We used green wool to outline how the spikes should link and then switched it out for stone after it looked correct. This should add an extra layer to the sides so everything blends together nicely.

CUSTOMIZATION OPTIONS

Bring your island to life with some simple scenery.

1 Now to add some cool buildings to our floating island. Up first, a simple house. Build the groundwork first from oak planks, oak wood, and stone bricks. The front side is five blocks across, the right corner is four up, then three to the right, the farthest right side is another row of five, and from here, you should be able to link it back onto itself.

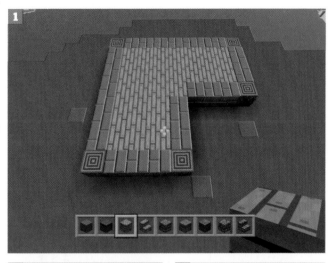

2 For the actual house, build all the walls up by four blocks. For the main walls, switch out stone for cobblestone and mossy cobblestone. Run spruce steps around the corner, then fill in the rest of the roof as you normally would. Add doors at the two five-wide sides, then one in the corner, and create a small garden area. Drop in steps at the two doors, fill the upper sections above the doors with oak planks, and you're done.

3 And for our lookout post, create a circle from stone bricks with the formation of three, one, three, one, three, one, three, one. Inside the circle, build four walls behind each of the three-wide sections. Build them up around ten blocks, then for the top sections, just rebuild a circle in line with the bottom circle and make it two blocks in height.

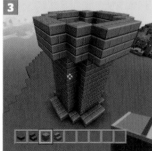

4 Knock out a doorframe at the bottom and add stone steps around the entrance along with fences with torches on them. For the top section, just build the single-block corners up by three, then add the roof with the help of stone brick half slabs. Head inside and run ladders going upward to the top, then when you reach the upper circle, lay down a floor.

5 This part is super important and helps bring everything together. Build a few random mounds from grass blocks. Pull out a tree sapling of your choosing (we went with oak) as well as bone meal. Plant saplings on the mounds and near the main house (feel free to extend the river if you want, too). Now dust the poor saps and the ground around them with bone meal and watch as your island comes to life.

09 NICE-LOOKING SIDES

Remember how we said earlier we'd be fixing up the sides? Well, now's the time to fix everything up. Look to the sides of the island. The idea here is to remove any corner blocks and replace them with either stone blocks or dirt blocks. If you find your dirt blocks are turning into grass blocks, just place a stone block above the dirt on the inside and it shouldn't sprout any grass.

10 RANDOM SHAPES

With the corners off, the sides still look a little too pristine, and we don't want "pristine," we want messy. For this, just place down random shapes onto the larger, flat sections, then more random blocks in the side areas. L shapes and other Tetris® formations work brilliantly, just don't overthink it too much. The less you focus on making this build perfect, the better the finished product will be. Weird, we know!

11 BRIGHTENING IT ALL UP

As you may have noticed, the underside is really dark. Like, a cave without a torch, dark. To fix this, we'll be dropping in some fireflies, although floating lanterns is probably more accurate. To build these little bundles of light, simply place either sea lanterns or glowstone with a slab above and below. Add in as many as you want. The beauty of these is they're small enough so you can place them anywhere it's dark and they don't look out of place.

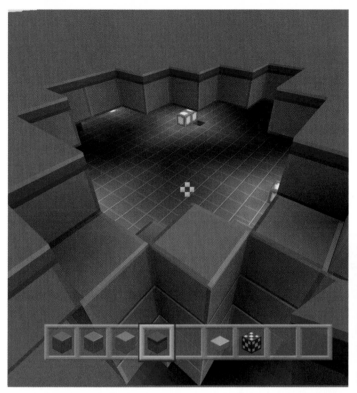

12
LAKE HOLE

Only two more sections to go, you got this! Head to the longest side, and knock out some of the corner sections. Continue knocking out blocks in a diagonal fashion until you've got a big enough hole. Now go into the hole and place dirt one block lower than ground level. Basically, we'll be filling the hole with water, so if you ever want to build anything on the inside, then you'll need to fill in the gap so water doesn't trickle inside.

BUILD BONUS

MORE INSPIRATION

Once you've got the basics of creating an island down, there's a lot of different builds you can try out. Instead of building one giant island, why not build several smaller platforms? You could even try your hand at building those ruined towers. All you've got to do is create a circle on the floor, build up the sides nice and high, add in the windows, then build a spiral roof. Oh, and add some foliage to make it look even more archaic.

13
MINI RIVER

Fill in the corner blocks once more to make a dam. Now fill the empty space with a water bucket. Here's the fun part. Once it's filled, smash out the corner blocks and watch as the water spills down to the water below. Not only do you have a small lake on your island, you've now also got a way of actually getting up there. Just remember, diving off the side into the ocean below is much more enjoyable than riding our watery elevation down!

MINI BUILDS

Build amazing things in ten minutes!

BUILD A HOMING BEACON

1 Make a *seriously* tall pillar out of a block of your choosing (we went with grass, for convenience). 4x4 blocks is wide enough for the beacon itself, but make sure that you lay a fifth block in each layer alongside this.

2 When your tower reaches the desired height, stand on that fifth stack of blocks, and delete the block beneath you. Add a ladder to the side of the main tower, then repeat these two steps until you reach the ground.

3 It's time to check that your work isn't going to be vain. In daylight, head off a decent distance from your beacon, and check that the tower is visible above any trees or obstacles around it.

4 Happy with the height of your beacon? Use the ladder to clamber back up to the top. Add a few layers of glowstone — these will serve as the light atop your beacon.

5 Whenever you're off exploring and need to find your way back, all you'll need to do is scan the horizon for your own personal lighthouse. And, as a bonus, the ladder means it can also double as a lookout tower!

BUILD A SPEEDY SHELTER

1 Going underground means you don't need to make walls, so we're heading downward for this shelter. To start, find a clear area and dig a 4x4 block crater one block deep.

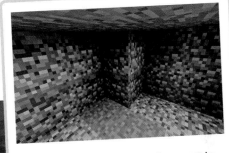

2 Excavate a farther two blocks down in the center of your crater. This is as deep as you'll need to go, and the shallower edges will mean you can get a roof over your head as quickly as possible.

3 Hop down into the deepest part of your shelter and add a roof above your head, working inward from the corners. We've used stone here, but almost any block will do in a pinch.

4 Place a torch or two in the corner to brighten things up, and then dig one block outward from each of the walls. You'll now have the 4x4 floor plan you originally laid out — just enough space for a one-night hideaway, should you ever need one.

5 Once you're holed up for the night, you might as well make the most of it. Place a crafting table and a bed — you can get in a few chores before hunkering down for a snooze until the sun rises in the morning.

69

MINI BUILDS

Build amazing things in ten minutes!

CONSTRUCT A SHOOTING RANGE

1 Build a target to your own design. We've gone for a very traditional pattern, but you can build a pattern to your own design.

2 To prevent mobs from crossing your line of sight while you're shooting, it's worth fencing in your range. Don't forget that you'll need a gate!

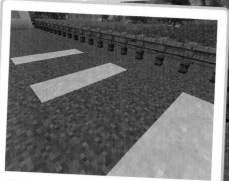

3 Set blocks into the ground to act as markers from which to shoot. You'll then need to place a few sets to help measure accuracy at different distances.

4 Add a chest and stock it with a few bows and plenty of arrows, so you always have practice materials on hand. Then draw your bow, line up, and work on hitting that target.

1 Create a frame that's 6x6 using chiseled stone bricks (or a block of your choice) and then place two extra blocks inside, as shown.

BUILD A STONE THRONE

2 Now fill the gap in the middle with a strong, rich color such as nether wart block or red nether brick.

4 Replace the corner blocks with gold ore (for added bling), then add some more chiseled stone blocks for the armrests.

3 Place four stone blocks at the back of the base, then six slabs of the same type in front of it. Stack four blocks then two stops above them.

BUILD A
DINO PARK

Keep your dinosaurs from running rampant!

ith the Better Together update now out in the wild, crafters have access to "Worlds." What is a world? Good question! Worlds are precrafted landscapes full of pre-made structures. In this case, Dinosaur Island comes with its own story mode, as well as dinosaurs (obviously!) and new behavior packs that make the dinosaurs act differently from other mobs.

In this guide, we will show you how to create your very own dinosaur park — complete with electric fences and a whopping great gate. If you don't have this world yet, never fear — just substitute the nether brick in this tutorial for the iron block and you can still make your own park (minus the dinosaurs, of course).

01
THE ROAD

Grab black and gray concrete, stone, and nether brick blocks. Dig up a five-wide trench and lay the blocks as shown. Next, extend the pattern by 15 blocks to create a road. You can add a rail to the center if you want your park to be a guided attraction. At the end of the road, build the two sets of 5x5 hollow rectangles. These rectangles are going to be the base of our main gate.

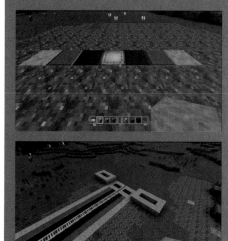

73

02

THE GATE

From the inner three-wide sides of the rectangle, extend the walls up by 12 blocks. Now build up the farthest-left wall by seven blocks, and fill in the middle with stone and nether brick (the nether bricks here act as markers for the next step). Then, in a diagonal formation, build the next walls up by two, then six, then four. After that, fill in the middle again with stone and place markers as shown.

03

THE OTHER SIDE

For this next part, we're going to be mirroring on the right side what we did on the left. So that's a diagonal formation of seven, two, six, and four. Then fill in the middle. Now for the redstone! Mine up the nether bricks and replace with netherrack. Then behind each block, lay redstone dust leading in to a redstone torch. Now grab metal pressure plates and add them to the netherrack, and watch as they magically clip into place.

04 THE HOLDING PENS

Create a four-high spike of stone half slabs, then continue the top two slabs across by seven blocks. Underneath the last slab, build it down. Add two-high cobblestone walls at each end with a slab on top. Then behind the structure, build two more half slab spikes going up by seven. Run cobble walls around the front, top, and back, then track iron fencing across the middle. Drop some redstone torches on top and finish with cobblestone behind the structure and iron fencing with slabs on top.

05
THE DOOR

To create our door, grab dark planks and a lighter plank of your choosing. At the back end of the gap in the middle of the gate, build two spikes from dark planks. Diagonally back from the first spikes, build two two-wide panels coming off one block lower than the spikes. Now you're free to build two single columns coming off the panel. Run the lighter wood through the middle, and the entrance to your dino park is now complete.

06
CONNECTING

Next up, we'll be connecting our first animal-pen panel to the entrance area. To do this, just mirror the first pen. Grab your stone half slabs again and continue the front section to the left and into the gate's wall. At the end, build it down, and add your cobblestone wall, then build the giant spike behind surrounded in more walls. It doesn't need to be the same width as the first, but it does need to have the same features.

07 MORE PEN WALLS

Okay, so these next few steps are going to be about building more of the animal-pen walls to create enclosed cages. Whatever you build on the left, you need to build exactly the same on the right. Each panel can be as long or short as you need, so don't worry about being precise, just as long as it's the same on the opposite side. With that in mind, build two more panels coming off both sides of the entrance gate.

08 CORNERS AND MORE

Corners can be tricky. You could just hack off the cobblestone wall and continue the panels along, but that will mess up the shape. Instead, add another long spike at the end of the wall, then plaster on cobblestone walls on the lower sections. You can even make a nice little "thing" out of one piece of iron fencing with half slabs above and below. And if your floor isn't level, just use the cobblestone wall formation in order to build downward onto uneven ground.

ICE-CREAM VAN

A good theme park needs delicious refreshments.

1 For this glorious delivery of delight, plop down two black wool blocks with a single gap between them. Then count five to the right and drop two more, and add buttons to the outer sides so that every block looks like a tire. Now grab some quartz half slabs and lay them down to create a flat surface on one block of either side of the wheels.

2 Decide which end you want to be the front, and place two inward-facing quartz steps with a netherrack block in between them. Then add a ladder to the rack's face. Behind each step, place a block of quartz. On the inner-side, run it along to the back then up and out for the window frame.

3 Head around to the other side of the van and build an upside down U shape at the front with a door in its center. To the right of this, using chiseled sand and pink, white, brown, and yellow wool, build the ice cream and the cone. For the back of the van, just place steps, glass pane, and upside down steps to create a back window.

4 Drop in more quartz steps along the front of the roof, then glass blocks underneath to act as the windshield. You can also add glass panes at the side of the glass blocks to create wing mirrors. Now head back to the big window hole and add levers on either side for the ice cream machine. Build a tray with your Neapolitan ice-cream–colored carpet on top.

5 Now all that's left to do is add a roof over the serving area. Use colored wool and item frames on the left and inside so people can see what's for sale, then build our giant cone on top out of wool, sandstone steps, and sandstone half slabs. Now when your dinosaur park visitors are parched, they will most certainly know where to go!

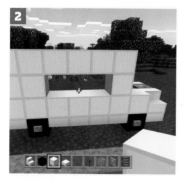

09
MORE BUILDING

This is an easy one. For the back side of our pen, simply run the double half slabs from one side so that they connect into the half slabs on the inner side. From here, you will be able to build the rest of the animal pen — the cobblestone, spikes, and so on — by just mimicking what you've done elsewhere in this tutorial. After the back side is complete, head around the right side of the gate and then build the pens on that side so it's symmetrical with the left side.

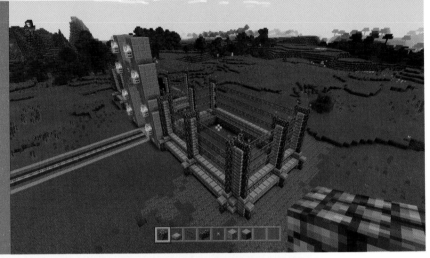

10
MORE PENS

Behind the front pen, this time on the right, build two more pens coming off. Try to have a rough idea of which dinosaurs you'll have in each. If you're going to house a T. rex or a Diplodocus, then you will need a large pen so they have space to move. Also, feel free to add more pens than just the two. Just keep it in your mind that you'll be copying the layout onto the opposite side.

11
OPPOSITE SIDE

Remember what we said about copying the layout on the opposite side? Well, guess what we'll be doing next. Building a house! Not really. We'll be copying the layout on the opposite side. So that's another two more pens behind the front pen. When you're done, you're now free to build the back wall interlinking the back two pens. That's all the time-consuming work out of the way, so next it's onto the easy stuff.

12
ROADS AND SIGNS

Take a look at the road leading through the doorway. We're now going to continue this road until we reach the back wall. Dig up a five-wide trench coming from the road all the way to the back, then fill it in with each of our road blocks. After that, grab a painting and keep cycling the picture until you get the restricted area signs. After all, you don't want anyone to wander in and get their arm bitten off.

BUILD BONUS

THE FOSSILS AND ARCHEOLOGY REVIVAL MOD

Available on PC, the Fossils and Archeology Revival Mod introduces a wealth of new content, including over 30 dinosaurs, a lush new landscape to explore, as well as a story mode which tasks the player with overthrowing an evil dictator. You can even find fossils underwater and use them to bring forgotten dinosaurs back to life. Another nice twist adds a mood function to dinosaurs, meaning if their mood is low, they might run off or attack you, or if it's high, they'll happily loiter around and not attack.

13
RELEASE THE DINOS

All that's left now is to grab some spawn eggs and drop your favorite dinosaurs into each of the animal pens. You could drop in some Triceratops, Diplodocuses, Tyrannosaurus rexes, Dilaphosaurus, Velociraptors — whatever you want! Just be careful with the Pterodactyls as they have a habit of flying off due to, you know, us not having a roof. Oh, and the really, really small dinosaurs can fit through the fence and leg it out into the open — the sneaky devils!

MINI BUILDS

Build amazing things in ten minutes!

BUILD AN IRON GOLEM

1 You don't want your Frankenstein's monster to get away, so you'll need a fence — whether that's blocks or a perimeter.

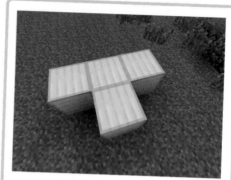

2 You'll need to place four blocks of tin on the ground a few blocks away from your fence, laid out in the shape of a capital T like so.

BUILD THIS!

3 Add a pumpkin or jack-o'-lantern block next to the middle block of the T, so that your blocks now form a cross shape. Your golem will then suddenly spring to life!

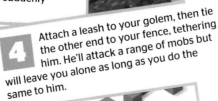

4 Attach a leash to your golem, then tie the other end to your fence, tethering him. He'll attack a range of mobs but will leave you alone as long as you do the same to him.

BUILD A MEDIEVAL LAMPPOST

1 Grab a wood block of your choice, then build a six-high spike. Now pull out the stone brick steps and place around the bottom.

2 Directly on top of the wooden spike, drop down a netherrack block. Underneath, run stone brick half slabs around the outside.

3 While looking at the netherrack, place upside down stone brick steps around the upper outside. When that's done, add netherrack fences on each step.

4 Now just place steps on top of the fences, a half slab in the center, and light the netherrack with a flint and steel.

MINI BUILDS!

Build amazing things in ten minutes!

CREATE YOUR OWN GIANT BOARD GAME

1 Mark out the board by laying colored blocks into the ground. An 8x8 board will give you plenty of space!

2 The best strategic view will be from above, so why not build a viewing platform from planks and stairs where you can consider your moves!

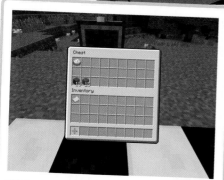

Connect Five
First to get a
line of five
WINS!

3 Place a chest beside the board and fill it with colored blocks of wool to use as counters. You can even add in prizes if you like!

4 If you have a particular game in mind, pop a sign alongside your game, and add some text to spell out the basic rules. This is an especially good plan if you're planning on constructing an entire arcade's worth of games!

1 You'll need to find a patch of fairly densely growing trees, ideally with flat canopies. A patch of jungle like this is the perfect locale.

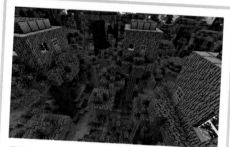

2 Build as many huts as you can fit, so everyone can have their own place to sleep and stash their gear. These can be as complex or simple as you like!

BUILD A NETWORK OF TREE HOUSES

3 Once your tree houses are built, it's time to link them together. Construct a walkway between the huts. It's a good plan to keep this fairly wide so nobody accidentally takes a tumble!

4 For an access point that blends into the surroundings, pile up jungle wood until it reaches your walkway, and clad it with vines for climbing. If you're worried about being able to find the access point from the bottom, you can plant some bright flowers around it.

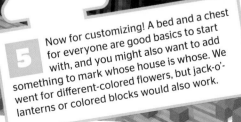

5 Now for customizing! A bed and a chest for everyone are good basics to start with, and you might also want to add something to mark whose house is whose. We went for different-colored flowers, but jack-o'-lanterns or colored blocks would also work.

THE JUNGLE MANSION

Living large in the middle of nowhere!

This one's all about building a honking great-big mansion for you and your friends to live in and then, if you so desire, destroying it. We'll show you the ins and outs of mansion building, as well as what to create in the surrounding area to really help bring it to life. When you're finished, you'll also have the option to turn it into a dilapidated ruin that looks like it hasn't seen an adventurer in hundreds of years. As with any massive build, you'll need a wide-open area to build on. If you're on a non-superflat world, just find a nice jungle and set fire to the trees to clear yourself some room.

01
THE FRONT AREA

Arm yourself with sandstone and quartz half slabs. Next, build a four-high, five-wide sandstone slab. One block back, drop in a two-wide slab coming from the left and right sides. Now go ahead and build nine separate spikes in a diagonal fashion coming from the two-wide slab. Run quartz slab around the bottom, then create the quartz railing going around the top edges by laying down a single row, then a row behind, then a top row above the first.

02
THE STAIRS

To the left of the last spike, build a two-wide slab that's one block lower than the spikes. Now build six more spikes in line with the two-wide slab. Run your half slab fencing across the top and bottom, then create a set of three-wide stairs. You could use quartz steps here, but making your own stairs out of half slabs lets you alter the height on the fly. When you're done, do the same on the opposite side (and keep it symmetrical).

03
FLOOR AND PILLARS

Pull out some polished diorite so we can get to work on the flooring. The plan here is to create a floor that's level with the fences. Just keep in mind that the left and the right sides should be slightly lower than the center section. Next create another set of stairs, then use a mixture of quartz pillar and quartz steps to create two five-high pillars. Note: The pillars should appear as four high due to covering the bottom block with steps.

04
THE PILLAR TOPS

Add another pillar block to your pillars, then connect with quartz half slabs. Next, run half slabs below and above the previous slabs. From here, run three slabs coming from the back and to the left. Then add a single block, turn, then add another three. Again, run slabs below and above. Add in the pillars as shown, then repeat this step on the opposite side. You should end up with six pillars in total.

05
WINDOWS AND WALLS

Before we get to installing windows, let's add in our guideline. In a straight line, from behind the back pillar, run a row of three sandstone, a two-wide gap, three more sandstone, another gap, then another three sandstone. From here, you can extend the walls up and down, fill the gaps with black panes, add slabs above and below, and use trapdoors to act as the wooden shutters. All you need to do now is drop a quartz spike at the end of the wall and run slabs along the top and bottom.

06
WALLS AND WINDOWS

Repeat the last step on the right side of the mansion. Directly behind the upper quartz slabs, create another wall with the same dimensions as the one below. Or just copy the lower wall by building it upward. Whatever's easiest! After that, build the central pillars up so you can see six blocks. Another quick note: If you're building this on survival, now is a good chance to clear out the surrounding area so we can fit the rest of the mansion behind these walls.

07 TOP OF THE PILLARS

Remember what we did with the pillars below? We'll be doing that again here. So, with quartz half slabs, connect the middle two pillars, then run slabs below and above to create that lovely depth. From here, run three slabs on the left and right, add a single lonely slab (aww), turn, then add another three. Add slabs below and above, and repeat this all on the right. Feel free to take a step back now and admire all your handiwork.

08 WALLS AND WALLS

This is the boring step. We know, we know, but every gigantic build has to have at least one bit that makes you want to pull your hair out. Better yet, call a friend over and get them to do this step. All they need to do is build the left and right walls (copy the window placement by following the blocks around) and the back wall, which we're leaving blank. When they're finished, you can go ahead and kick them out.

JUNGLE-IFYING THE MANSION
Welcome to the jungle (mansion)

1 You're mansion isn't exactly a jungle mansion yet. Pull out some vines and a leaf block of your choosing. Now just go to town and place them everywhere! For the best sweeping plants, run leaf blocks over the edges of the upper sections and build straight down to ground level.

2 Now head inside and onto the upper floor. Place TNT near the front wall, in the middle of the floor, and in the corner. Explode it to give the mansion that ruined feeling. And as with the last step, run vines and leaf blocks everywhere so it looks like the green is reclaiming the inside.

3 Go back outside and look to the farther right side. Use several TNTs to blow up most of the corner, but not all of it — leave the bottom section. Grab the blocks you'd use to fix it and drop them randomly at the base so it looks like the wall has collapsed. And, of course, add more vines.

4 Head inside to the lower floor (you can also set your time to night for added spookiness). To make it look like various travelers have sought shelter here, make a firepit from stone half slabs, then drop netherrack in the center and light it (netherrack always stays lit). Blow out the back wall as well, just because it looks cool.

5 All that's left now is to head back outside one last time and plant a selection of trees. You can use whichever tree you like, but we opted for dark spruce saplings, which, by the way — need to be placed in a 2x2 formation otherwise they won't grow when you dust them with bone meal. And with that, you're free to sit back and bask in our mansion's ruined beauty!

09
THE ROOF, THE ROOF

Hopefully your friend isn't too mad with you for kicking them out. Anyway . . . equip with stone bricks and stone brick half slabs. Now, with quartz half slabs, create the outline of the roof. If you use quartz steps here, your roof is going to look ridiculously big — hence we're using half slabs. Behind the slabs, switch to your stone brick slabs and run them across the entire roof. When you reach the end, swap out the bricks for the quartz again.

10
FRONT ROOF

Head back around to the front and turn the upper-pillar's slab section into a rectangular shape that feeds into the roof. Using the upper section as the bottom of the roof, create the diamond shape at the front. Again, use quartz half slabs to control the height. Now all that's left to do is run stone brick half slabs from behind and into the roof, then at the front, create a smaller window from quartz blocks.

11
FRONT DOORS

Head back down to the lower-pillar sections and fill in the floor with sandstone and sea lanterns. Now build in the wall, add a door, and create shaped windows from brown clay and black glass. Do the same above, only this time using sandstone steps to fashion a different style of window. You can also head inside and build the flooring and ceiling, also from brown clay. But be warned, the floor and ceiling will take you a while. Have you and your friend made up yet?

12
ROADS AND SIGNS

We're now nearing the finishing line. All that's left is the flooring outside and a posh fountain. For the floor, use your quartz half slabs to connect the side of the mansion with the outer side of the steps down the front. From here, you'll be able to fill in the floor. Just keep in mind, the floor will be (intentionally) different levels. To blend the jumps, just lay down quartz half slabs and connect them into the sides and the staircase.

NEXT LEVEL!

AWESOME VICTORIAN MANSION

One crafter by the name of WastedGamer has put together a tutorial of how to create a pretty sweet Victorian mansion. The rough idea here is to build circular towers interlinking with one another. What's also equally impressive is the mansion's interior builds. WastedGamer has spent a lot of time meticulously crafting realistic living rooms, kitchens, studies, and more. And if you're on a PC and don't want to spend weeks painstakingly re-creating this monster build, there's always the option to download it and check it out yourself.

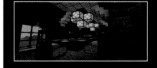

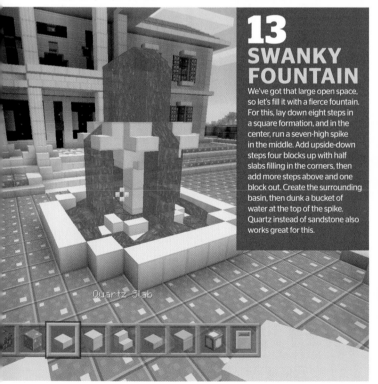

13
SWANKY FOUNTAIN

We've got that large open space, so let's fill it with a fierce fountain. For this, lay down eight steps in a square formation, and in the center, run a seven-high spike in the middle. Add upside-down steps four blocks up with half slabs filling in the corners, then add more steps above and one block out. Create the surrounding basin, then dunk a bucket of water at the top of the spike. Quartz instead of sandstone also works great for this.

Quartz Slab

91

MINI BUILDS

Build amazing things in ten minutes!

BUILD AN EASY BOAT DOCK

1 Place four wooden slabs on blocks next to water. Build a walkway of wooden planks that is 16 blocks long and four wide.

2 Break the plank in its corners. Break two more planks on each side, then build a block column in each of the gaps that's one block above the walkway and drops to the seabed.

3 Place four fence posts between the first and second set of wooden blocks, and then place one fence post on each side of every other wood block.

BUILD THIS!

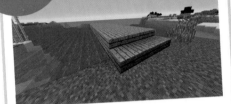

4 Build boat docking spots using wooden slabs in the areas where there is no fence, four long by two wide. Slot your boats in. Light the area with glowstone lamps covered in trapdoors. Then your boat dock will be complete!

BUILD THE BLACKSMITH FORGE

1 Create a 3x3 square from stone bricks, then replace the front row with steps. Next add more steps on top of the three other sides of the forge.

2 Add inward-facing steps at the middle of the three sides, single blocks on the inside corners, then one more step on the front-left.

3 From the step at the front, curve more steps around the front, then connect them back in and around the edges.

4 Inside the cross section, place lava on the floor, then use stone bricks to build four pillars vertically. Add steps at the top and then you're finished.

MINI BUILDS!

Build amazing things in ten minutes!

A CRUMBLING PVP ARENA

1 Mark boundaries for the arena by laying blocks, slabs, and stairs in a circle. For two players, build at least 25 blocks across.

2 Build three walls with stairs up to the top for starting zones. Add cover blocks on top. Mix up the shapes and sizes of the areas.

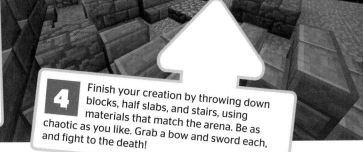

3 Build obstacles between the structures, such as arches, smaller walls, and pillars to climb up.

4 Finish your creation by throwing down blocks, half slabs, and stairs, using materials that match the arena. Be as chaotic as you like. Grab a bow and sword each, and fight to the death!

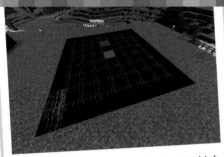

1 Till a square of grass blocks, nine high and nine wide. Dig out the center square and pour in water. Wait for the tilled blocks to darken so that they are ready for planting in your farm.

A COMPACT TWO-PERSON FARM

2 Build a fence around the plot, ensuring there are no gaps between the tilled dirt and the fence posts. Jungle wood looks good here, we reckon. Don't forget to add an access gate!

3 Pick a crop — we chose melons and pumpkins! Add two rows of melon seeds with a two-row gap in the middle. Repeat with pumpkin seeds. Plant a third crop to divide them.

4 Wait for your crops to grow, and harvest at your leisure. If you're bored with pumpkin and melon, swap in different seeds and plant four rows instead of two. Remember to keep that middle dividing line, though!

BUILD A BOEING 737

Take to the skies in your very own airplane!

Don't tell anyone this, but building an airplane isn't actually that hard. It's time-consuming, sure, but surprisingly straightforward once you know what you're doing. The trick is to get the main body, the fuselage, out of the way first, then get a solid guideline in place for the other sections of the airplane. Once your guideline is correct, the rest just falls into place.

We'll also be showing you how to fill the inside of your Boeing 737 to make it as realistic as possible and how to build a working engine. Just keep in mind that engines are quite noisy, so maybe turn the volume down just a bit.

01
THE FUSELAGE

Let's start by building a circle from quartz. Keep the main lengths at five, and the diagonal sections at two. Next comes the long-winded part. We'll be building from behind the circle by 65 blocks. Start with each of the five-tall sections, build them back by 65, then complete the remaining four sets of two. Don't worry if you lose count; so long as it's around 65-ish, you'll be fine.

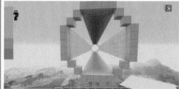

02
THE FRONT CONE PART 1

Pick an end to be the front. Find the center of the top row then build out by five blocks. Add one three-long section diagonally below, then another two, two-long platforms. Next create a sideways T shape at the end. Mirror the above only in reverse to connect to the bottom of the circle. Now repeat this process two more times on the horizontal axis. This weird shape is the skeleton of the front of the plane.

03 THE FRONT CONE PART 2

Head back to the center at the top of the circle and place three blocks on each side of the five-long section. From here, place blocks in the same formation, only diagonally down from the last one. Keep doing this until you reach the middle. Repeat this on the bottom, then on the sides. Knock out an area for the windshield before filling it with black glass blocks (make sure you use blocks and not panes, as panes will not look good here).

04 THE TAIL

First, knock out the corners on the fuselage. Now head to the back end and place a row of seven coming from the bottom-center of the circle. Add more rows in a diagonal fashion with the lengths of five, four, three, three, two, two, one. Add in a 3x3 plate at the top of the last row. To finish, just run a row from the top of the plate back to the center-top of the circle.

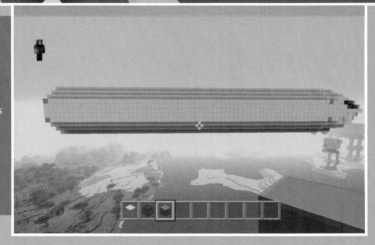

05
THICKENING THE TAIL END

Begin by thickening the lower line so it's three blocks in width. Now for the tricky part. Build more zigzag lines diagonally one block out. Keep doing this until you reach halfway, then build from the circle so it all connects. Check both sides to make sure they're all lining up right, then blend the newest section into the fuselage. When done, add a quartz strip below as shown. Do keep in mind, this may take a few attempts, so don't get discouraged if it's not perfect.

06 THE TAIL

You should currently be looking at a very strange, eel-like plane. So let's start making it more "planey." At the back, build four, four-high diagonal pillars. In front of that, build the formation as shown in the image. The individual lengths are four out, then heading back down to the plane, one, one, two, one, two, one, two, one two, one, two, one, two. After you've built the spine, feel free to fill it all in.

07
MINI WINGS

Pull out some quartz half slabs and run a row of 11 along the side of the fuselage. Build one out from the right side, then two, then another two. For the next two sections, build it one block higher. Continue building what's in the image (the green blocks show where you need to go up by a block) before heading to the left side of the row and building out again. And, of course, build another wing on the opposite side.

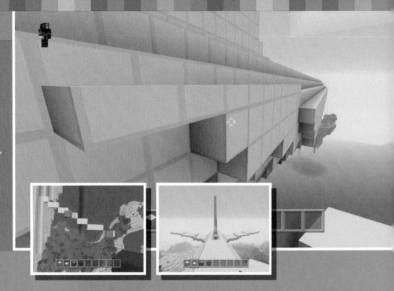

08
THE MAIN WINGS

Now that you've got the hang of building the mini wings, it's time to build the main two wings. Start with an L shape coming from around the middle of the fuselage. Build in sets of three, and on every third set, build one block up on the farthest two blocks. Keep doing this until you've got a good width, then repeat the process to join it up. After you've filled the space in between, make the wings two deep up until the final two sections.

THE ENGINE

Build a working engine to give your plane a more authentic feel.

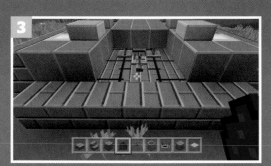

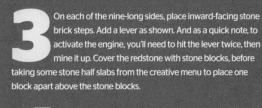

1 You can build this engine wherever you like. Inside the plane, on top of the plane, below; anywhere! So it's easier to see, we'll be building it on the ground. Start by placing stone bricks in an 11x9 formation. Chop off the corners and fill in the floor.

2 Next up, we'll be wiring the redstone circuit so when it's turned on, it makes a lot of noise, just like a real engine. Place four repeaters in a square, all on two ticks. Connect them together with redstone dust, then create four prongs coming off. At the end of these prongs, place sticky pistons facing up. Pull out iron blocks and dump them on top of the pistons.

3 On each of the nine-long sides, place inward-facing stone brick steps. Add a lever as shown. And as a quick note, to activate the engine, you'll need to hit the lever twice, then mine it up. Cover the redstone with stone blocks, before taking some stone half slabs from the creative menu to place one block apart above the stone blocks.

4 Head around to the back of the engine and draw a stone brick cross in the middle of the seven-long section. Build this cross so it's two blocks deep. Add stone brick steps in the corners to make it look slightly smaller than what we'll be building next. Grab some black wool and build a 3x3 square behind the cross. Add a backward-facing dispenser and you're almost done.

5 Run two strips of black wool coming from the cross alongside the stone half slabs. Now for a neat trick. Add in skeleton skulls/masks atop the black wool to create a kind of knobbly effect. It's crazy, but it works surprisingly well. Place steps in front of the black wool; and along the front of the engine, replace the lower bricks with slabs.

09
ENGINES

A plane can't fly without engines. So let's fix that. Build a quartz circle toward the outermost part of the wing. Make it three deep, then build a smaller circle inside from gray wool. Fill behind the smaller circle with black wool and add a backwards dispenser. Now make another smaller circle behind the black from dark gray wool and build it back. At the back of the plane, build a three-deep smaller circle from quartz and add in black wool and another dispenser.

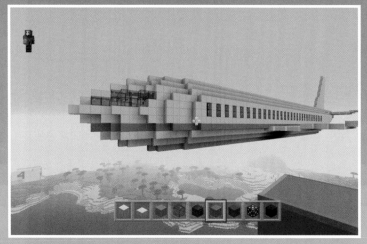

10
ADD SOME COLOR

Pick a colored wool you like. We went with teal because teal is awesome! From the front of the plane, mine in and run a strip of wool going around. Drop in some windows while you're here, too. When you reach the back end, start mining diagonally upward. The goal here is to cover that back half of the fin on top. When that's all finished, do the same on the opposite side so it matches up.

11 SEATING AREA

Chuck some iron doors in at the front, leading to the cockpit, and near the center of the wing. Head inside and create a flat surface from your chosen wool and a lighter shade. Add in rows of stone brick steps, too (so they look like chairs), then build the ceiling inward by a few rows. This will allow you to put in some sea lanterns and build around it so it all blends nicely.

12 RESTROOMS

At the very back of our seating area, create a narrow passage with four sets of doors, two on each side. Behind each of the doors, build a wall to separate each of the cubicles. As for the toilets themselves, place down a cauldron filled with water. Add an iron trapdoor above, with two quartz blocks behind. Lay a single piece of white carpet on top of the quartz, a button for the flusher, and carpet around the toilet.

BUILD BONUS

HOW TO TAKE TO THE SKIES FOR REAL

If there's one thing Minecraft needs, it's the ability to actually take builds airborne. With the Minecraft Flight Simulator mod for PC, you can do just that. This mod pack comes with a host of ready-made airplanes that, once you've got them fueled up, can be used to soar around the world.

Unlike other flying mod packs, when your plane runs out of fuel, it doesn't just drop to the ground like a brick balloon. Instead, the plane slowly veers downward, allowing the pilot, if they're talented enough, to perform a crash landing to avoid going splat. Not bad, eh?

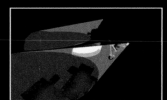

13 THE COCKPIT

All that's left to do now is our cockpit area. Section off the wall leading to the carriage with two doors and quartz. At the front of the plane, under the glass windshield, lay down some stone brick steps with a block behind, a redstone repeater, two levers — in front and above — and some half slabs with buttons under them. Now just head outside and add the wheels if you so desire and your Boeing 737 is complete!

MINI BUILDS

Build amazing things in ten minutes!

BUILD A FISHING PLATFORM

1 First, you need to lay a platform. Once you've picked your waterside fishing spot, lay down a 3x4 platform of wooden blocks alongside the shore — we went for birch planks to match the sand.

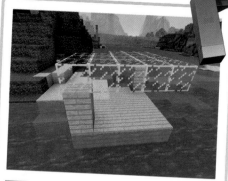

2 Who wants to get wet in the rain? Not us! We have used glass blocks here in order to create a roof that will still let plenty of sunlight through while you are trying to catch yourself some lunch.

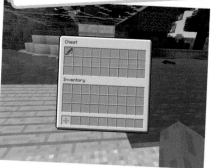

3 If you're always going to be returning to the same spot, it doesn't make sense to keep lugging your gear about, so pop a chest down in your shelter to store your fishing rod.

4 Finally, why not add a furnace so you can cook up what you catch. You can keep fuel on hand in your chest from Step 3. Goodbye to sushi, hello to fish and chips!

BUILD A RACETRACK

1 You'll need to lay out your ideal track — we did this by inlaying red sand blocks on a patch of clear grass. Keeping your track about three blocks wide is ideal, and be careful not to make corners too tight.

2 Fencing in your track means that nobody can cheat by cutting corners or sneakily overtaking anyone on the outside of the track. Not that we would ever do such dastardly things, of course . . .

4 Tame two or three horses that you find in the wild, then saddle them up and ride them on over to your track. You're now all set to start competing (and winning) in your own miniature Kentucky Derby!

3 Use some grass path blocks or hay bales to create jumps. Spread them the width of the track, but make sure you don't place them right on the corners; otherwise your course will be too difficult to be fun!

MINI BUILDS

Build amazing things in ten minutes!

CREATE AN ICE RINK

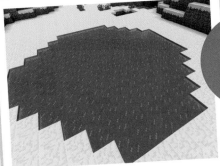

1 Find yourself a nice, flat section of snowy ground, and lay out your rink by inlaying blocks of ice. You can make this as large or small as you like, and in any shape.

2 Ice is very slippery, so place some fencing around the perimeter of your rink to stop people from flying off. You can leave gaps in this at the corners so people can easily get in.

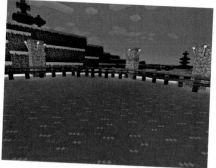

3 Skating at twilight is lovely and very atmospheric, but you'll need some lighting to do this. Most light sources actually *melt* ice, so ensure that you place your torches a few blocks up off of the ground and away from the ice!

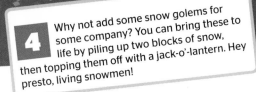

4 Why not add some snow golems for some company? You can bring these to life by piling up two blocks of snow, then topping them off with a jack-o'-lantern. Hey presto, living snowmen!

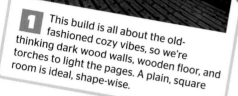

HOW TO BUILD A LIBRARY

1 This build is all about the old-fashioned cozy vibes, so we're thinking dark wood walls, wooden floor, and torches to light the pages. A plain, square room is ideal, shape-wise.

2 A library is quite literally not a library without copious amounts of printed words, so place a number of bookshelves around the walls of your room.

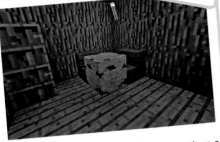

3 To make a cozy reading corner, place a wooden block to serve as a table, and make "chairs" by surrounding the table with segments of wooden stairs. We added a cake, too — why not, eh?

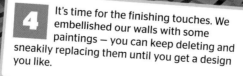

4 It's time for the finishing touches. We embellished our walls with some paintings — you can keep deleting and sneakily replacing them until you get a design you like.

BUILD A
HANSEL AND GRETEL SWEET HOUSE

Lure foes and eat cake.

ave you read the story of _Hansel and Gretel?_ Don't. It's really messed up. That said, the idea of a house made entirely of devilishly delicious sweets is too great an idea to pass up when you're a master builder! For this guide, the candy texture pack is a must. If you don't own it, though, that's not a problem. Simply build the house with the correct blocks in whichever texture pack you desire, then afterward, load it back up in the sweet texture pack. You won't be able to save, but you'll be able to view the house as it was meant to be seen.

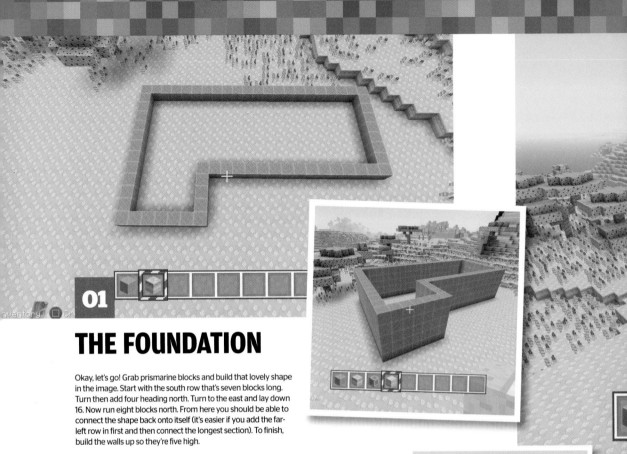

01 THE FOUNDATION

Okay, let's go! Grab prismarine blocks and build that lovely shape in the image. Start with the south row that's seven blocks long. Turn then add four heading north. Turn to the east and lay down 16. Now run eight blocks north. From here you should be able to connect the shape back onto itself (it's easier if you add the far-left row in first and then connect the longest section). To finish, build the walls up so they're five high.

02 THE UPPER SECTION

Next grab dirt blocks. On top of the bottom layer of the house, count out by one block, then run dirt blocks all the way around the outside. When you view the house from above, you should still be able to see the prismarine blocks from the first step. Once you've gone around, drop in two more rows of dirt on top of the first layer so the upper section is now four blocks in height. Finally, use stone brick steps to create the step formation shown.

03
THE ROOF

Now it's time to plop on the chocolate roof. On the farthest left side, continue the steps until they reach the back. On the smaller right side at the front, run the steps to where the corner meets the next wall. Next head to the farthest right side and create another step formation there. Connect the step formation along the front so it attaches to the smaller section of the roof, and then scoot around the back and finish that side.

04 OREOS

Hungry yet? Does anyone else really, really, really crave a slice of cake? For this next part, arm yourself with stone slabs. Run a two-high strip around the outside, then a single strip in front. Grab some purpur pillar and mine up the corners and replace them. Pop a door in the middle of the front section with windows to the sides and above. And finally, pull out some iron bars and place them around the doorframe and above it.

WINDOWS

It's window-building time! Equip ladders and pink stained glass. Looking to the right of the windows, on the second largest side, count two blocks in. Place two ladders, knock out a 2x3 hole, and replace with glass. Then two more ladders. Miss a block, then repeat the window formula once more. Now head to the farthest left side and build a third window in the center.

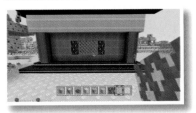

06
UPPER WINDOW

With those three windows out of the way, all we need now is a window on the upper section, above the door. For this we'll be using note blocks (which look like marshmallow!) and more pink stained glass. Find the center and knock out a 2x2 hole. Place the glass panes one block back to add some depth, then you can knock out a two-high column on either side of the window and lay down your note blocks.

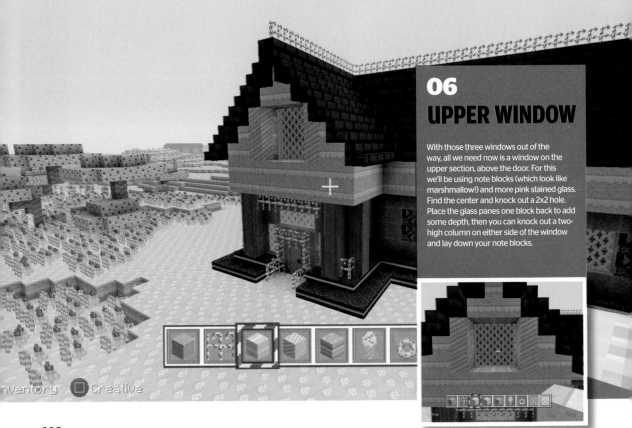

DON'T OWN THE CANDY PACK?

Although the candy pack is an important part of making a house made from sweets, with a few changes, you can turn this build into a neat little house. First, replace the upper dirt section with spruce planks and change out the prismarine blocks for oak planks. Next look to all the purpur pillars and the note blocks. Now smash them all to pieces. In their place, add in columns of jungle wood. For the windows, break them all and add white glass panes. For the window shutters on the sides, do away with the ladders and use banners instead. And just like that, you've transformed a candy home into a completely different house with just a few switches.

07

THE BLUE PATH

Next we need to lay down a very inviting path to lure unsuspecting foes to our candy house. Our house looks the part, but how will people find it when we start adding trees? For this, grab a grass path block, dig up a two-wide trench from the front of the house leading away, and then fill it in. Underneath the iron bars by the front door, use sandstone as the underside, seeing as iron bars don't sit correctly on grass paths.

08 FLOWER POWER

In the candy texture pack, every single one of the flowers has been replaced with mouth-watering lollipops and candy treats. Fill your hotbar with seven flowers of your choice, and make the eighth one the tall cotton candy. Coming from the door, place one cotton candy on each side of the path. Now run a selection of the other flowers until the end, where you finish on another set of cotton candy. Delicious!

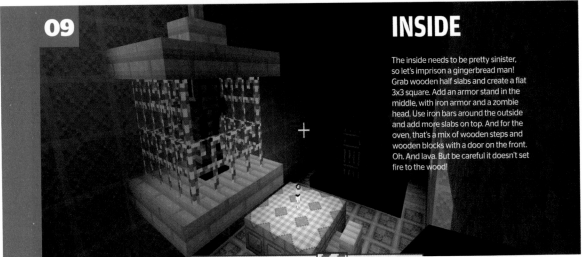

09

INSIDE

The inside needs to be pretty sinister, so let's imprison a gingerbread man! Grab wooden half slabs and create a flat 3x3 square. Add an armor stand in the middle, with iron armor and a zombie head. Use iron bars around the outside and add more slabs on top. And for the oven, that's a mix of wooden steps and wooden blocks with a door on the front. Oh. And lava. But be careful it doesn't set fire to the wood!

10 FINISHING TOUCHES

It's the homestretch. All that's left to do is turn the surrounding area into a nice but creepy woodland area. Pull out a tree sapling of your choosing. (Also in the candy texture pack, you have the choice of a selection of ice-cream trees!) Next, grab some bone meal. Dot the saplings around the outside of the house that you've just constructed, but not on the path. When you've got enough use bone meal, watch as they turn fully-sized trees.

OTHER OVEN

Building a different oven that lights itself

Of course, in *Hansel and Gretel*, the wicked witch was fattening up the two children for dinner but ended up in the oven herself. Better put one in, then, in case some candy-loving mobs come to visit …

1 How about an oven that works like a real one? Sounds good? Cool. Let's do this. Dig up a 2x3 hole. Place redstone dust in the front section and upward-facing dispensers along the back. Now add a flint and steel to each dispenser. The flint and steel will be responsible for lighting the oven.

2 Next, pull out some furnaces from the creative menu. Line them up in a row of three on top of the redstone dust. Now add buttons to the front of each of them. On top of each furnace, add a pressure plate. The buttons will be in charge of lighting the fire, but if you chuck an item on top of the furnace, like a pork chop, that, too, will help to light them.

3 Equip sandstone, sandstone steps, and sandstone half slabs. You can use other blocks, but make sure they're nonflammable! Run a row of sandstone blocks around the outside of the device — on the left and right sides and behind. Next, with your steps, drop them to the left and right of the sandstone, and then on top.

4 Drop in another few blocks of sandstone at the back so it becomes level with the steps on the left and right sides. Now go ahead and use your half slabs to cover the gap and create a hood above the dispensers. The half slabs should allow you to still see the flames when they're lit.

5 Connect the steps on the left and right sides with another row of steps in the middle. Now all that's left to do is use your sandstone blocks to create a chimney coming from the top. Because the structure is made from nonflammable blocks, it's completely safe to keep inside the house because it won't set your wooden sections on fire. Hooray!

MINI BUILDS

Build amazing things in ten minutes!

CREATE A WOLF KENNEL

1 Use some wooden blocks to build a small structure. You don't really need to worry about a door — an open front will do — but using some colored wool blocks as a floor will give your canine chum some much-needed comfort.

2 Sure, you *could* tie your wolf up, but putting a fence around the kennel means you won't need to. Why not leave a few blocks around the building itself so they have got some space to run around?

BUILD THIS!

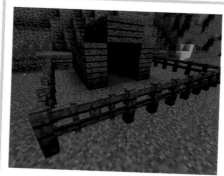

3 Cooping up an animal without a water bowl is downright inhumane, so remove one grass block and fill in the space using a water bucket. Voilà — instant drinking bowl!

4 Add a sign just beside the fence with your mutt's name as decoration, and let them loose in their very own kennel enclosure — just don't forget to shut the gate behind you!

CREATE A WATER FEATURE

1 It's a really good idea to start with an existing hill for this particular build. At the bottom, dig out a small pool, then add in a set of steps carved into the ground behind it.

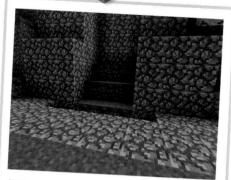

2 Once your basic structure is in place, use stone blocks (we went for moss stone to make it look aged) to pave around your water feature.

BUILD THIS!

3 Clamber up to the top of your soon-to-be waterfall, and empty water buckets into the pool until it's full. It's best to start in the middle and then work to either side.

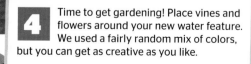

4 Time to get gardening! Place vines and flowers around your new water feature. We used a fairly random mix of colors, but you can get as creative as you like.

MINI
BUILDS

Build amazing things in ten minutes!

HOW TO BUILD A SPACESHIP DESTROYER

1 Start by building a 5x5 cuboid from light gray wool. Chop off the corners, then add an iron trapdoor on top.

2 At the front, create a cross section with black glass. Add steps and half slabs, then use gray wool on the inside for the cockpit.

3 Next create two cross sections on each side. Build out by two, then form a 3x3 panel with blocks poking out on each side of the cockpit.

4 To finish, make circles behind the panels with the main length of five blocks. Add in the details, then fill the gaps with gray wool.

1 Begin with a 3x3 flat quartz panel. Then use the half slabs to build the front, then wool and some more slabs behind to create the body.

HOW TO BUILD A USS EXPLORER

2 Create a quartz-and-stone box behind the body to make the inside. Next, add a hatch to the cockpit. Build the inside, then cover with glass.

3 Use steps for the start of the wings, then slabs to lengthen them. For the thrusters, place stone brick steps to form a cross-like shape.

4 Now just run quartz slabs on the underside, along with a row of stone at the back, and you're done.

119

THE GIANT TREE

A treemendous tree to tower over your world.

Do you wanna build a tree house? Come on, let's go and build! Making a tree house is a good way to spend time in Minecraft. But what if you want to not just build a tree house, but a giant tree with several houses dangling off its branches? In this guide we'll be showing you how to go about building a giant tree, step by step. The trick is to not build it straight, otherwise you end up with a massive, wooden rocket. Adding curves helps, as does getting the roots and branches right. Also, if you've got the City Texture pack, slap it on, because it really does house some luscious tree skins.

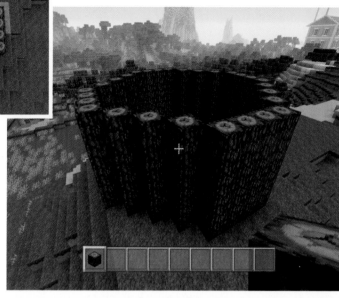

01
THE BASE CIRCLE

Grab yourself your favorite wood block. We used spruce wood, but feel free to use whichever you like. Go ahead and lay down a row of four horizontally, and followed by three diagonally up, then four up, three up left, four left, three down left, four down, and three down right to connect the shape. This should form a circle. When that's done, build up all the stubs by an additional five blocks so they're nice and tall.

02
TO THE SIDE

See that lime terra-cotta? Notice how the whole circle is one block to the right? Build that, only instead of using lime terra-cotta, use your wood block. When the circle is in place, build up this section by four blocks. We'll be doing quite a bit of moving the circle in different directions to give our tree some shape, so if you find it causes any gaps, just fill them in with your wood block.

03
MORE
SECTIONS

What we just did in the last part covers what we're going to be doing for the next few steps. With that in mind, build another circle one block to the right, and build it up by three. Now build another circle, but this time cut the corners down to just two blocks (keep the straight rows as four). Fill in the gaps to the left, then build your newest section so that it's five blocks in height.

04
EVEN MORE
SECTIONS

This step will cover the next five sections. Start by laying down your circle, again one block to the right, and build a two-high section. Repeat the process to create a four-high section and two more two-high sections. Drop down one last circle, then build it up by seven blocks. That's the main bulk of the tree completed; now all that's left is for you to curve the tree in the opposite direction.

05
CHANGE IN DIRECTION

Now for the last part of the shaft: the final four sections. Start by plopping down your circle, but instead of dropping it one block to the right, drop it one block to the left. Fill in any gaps that may appear, then build up the wall by two blocks. Repeat this process to create the last three sections, which are three blocks high, followed by two blocks, then seven blocks to finish. Now take a step back and admire your terrific tree shaft.

06
ROOTS

While our shaft is complete, there's still some work to do before it's a full-fledged tree. Head down the base of the shaft, and with your wood block, trace different lines across the ground. Don't worry about it looking perfect, for now we'll be going in and making our guidelines thicker until they resemble real roots. Running them along the ground works, but for added effect, try elevating them slightly.

07
BRANCHES

With our roots in place, we'll now be venturing to the top to add some branches. Go to the four-wide part of the top circle and, just like we did with the roots, build a thin, random shape coming off. Be sure to make this have a curved shape, otherwise it won't look like a tree! Now keep thickening the shape you created until it looks like a branch.

08
FINISHING THE WOOD

Go ahead and build at least three branches in total, all of which should be on different sides. Don't worry if your tree isn't identical to ours (creating a mirror image of a tree build is impossible). When you're happy with how your branches and roots look, go back to the top and fill in the gap. This doesn't need to be neat since we'll be adding some foliage in a few steps, so no one will see it anyway.

CONSTRUCT A TREE BEDROOM

Turn the inside of your tree into a swanky bedroom

1 Begin by heading down to the base of the tree and finding one of the four-long walls. Smash a two-high space, then with cobblestone steps, half slabs, and blocks, create the doorframe. Start by putting the steps in place, then add in the half slabs above the opening before placing the solid blocks to finish this section.

2 Next up, we need a bed, because what's the point in making a bedroom if there isn't anywhere to sleep? For this, equip some spruce half slabs and spruce steps. Oh, and beds, obviously. Lay down two beds next to each other along the back wall, then drop half slabs around them. Run spruce two blocks out from the top, then fill in the sides, and that's it.

3 Yes, we need a TV area. How else are we going to pretend to play video games inside a video game? To build the sofa, grab some purpur steps and place two down, facing away from the wall. Now place one at each end so they curve. As for the TV, that's just a painting in the City Texture pack. If you don't own this pack, use any old painting and it'll still look like a TV.

4 Now for some storage options. Mine two blocks out of the ceiling above an empty wall. Grab your spruce wood and build a U shape. There should be a two-block gap in the middle just below the ceiling. On the bottom rung of the U, which is two blocks across, place down two doors of your choosing. Open the doors and replace the back blocks with spruce, and then you've got yourself a simple working cupboard!

5 All that's left to finish the bedroom at the base are some decorative measures. Try using gray glazed terra-cotta for the walls as it really does look like wallpaper. Have a play with your paintings, too (our air vents are actually just paintings). Use stone for the ceiling and embed sea lanterns for some much-needed light. Use black carpet for the flooring, and you've got yourself one swanky pad.

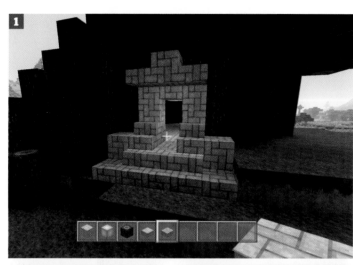

09 VILLAGER HOUSE

At the end of each of the branches, run oak fences in a vertical line heading downward. About ten fences should do it. Now let's build a simple, hanging villager house. Create a 5x5 flat square from your wood block below the fencing. Then, using cobblestone and oak planks, create the four-wide cuboid as shown here. Add the door and glass panes, then create a mini path going around the base.

10 HOUSE THE SECOND

Place a 5x5 flat square of dirt around the bottom fencing on your second branch. Build another 5x5 cuboid, then chop the corners off to add a bit of shape. Run steps around the top and plant a crop of your choosing on the roof. Now pull out some stone half slabs and dot them around the bottom, and below the top steps. Throw in a door, and that's this mini house complete.

11 ONE MORE HOUSE

And for our last house, drop a 5x5, flat oak square at the bottom of the third branch's fencing. Equip spruce steps and spruce half slabs, then create the step roof. Don't worry if it covers the fencing; that can be easily fixed when you're finished. Add in the row of spruce wood, then build the underneath. Use glass panes on the side and for the door, and cover the inner frame with oak fence. Create the small balcony in front, and you're almost finished.

12
LEAVES

Head into the creative menu and equip some jungle leaves (or whichever is your favorite leaf block). Go to the branches and run a row of leaves along the middle topside of each. Place leaves to the left and right of the strip, then build them up by two or three blocks. Fill the center area at the top of the shaft, build that area up, and your tree is finally realistic enough to be considered a real tree!

13
EXTRA TIPS

Now all that's left to do is a small bit of housekeeping. Add more leaf blocks in between the branches at the top so the upper area has an almost dome-like appearance. Next, do you see the multiple flat areas on the shaft of the tree? Let's give it some shape by running straight vertical lines up that space, as well as random shapes. And with that, your giant tree is complete. Just be sure to keep your flint and steel far, far away!

EXISTING FOREST

BUILD A TREE HOUSE KINGDOM

If building your own tree from scratch isn't your thing, why not build a tree house kingdom in an existing forest? The idea behind this build is to first find a massive jungle biome, then grab as much wood as you can possibly carry. If you have an open area, build in there; if not, just build on top of the trees. The houses are created via a similar circle foundation, just like in our build. The only difference being they've been turned into homes rather than a giant tree. You could even steal the idea of connecting all the houses with fencing to create interlinking platforms.

100% UNOFFICIAL!

Games Master PRESENTS

STAY ALIVE IN MINECRAFT

TIPS FOR DEFEATING CREEPERS, SPIDERS, MONSTERS, AND MORE!

INSIDE YOU WILL FIND

DETAILED DIARIES   BRILLIANT BUILDS   COOL CREATURES   TOP TIPS & TRICKS

ESCAPE FROM VILLAINS

PLAN YOUR ATTACKS

SURVIVE 'TIL THE END

CREATE COOL DEFENSES

The world of Minecraft is full of wonder, discovery, and most of all, fun! But it can also be dangerous, even for the most battle-hardened players. This book will keep you one step ahead of all the mobs and creepers who might try to bring your adventures to a deadly end.

■ Tips and tricks to stay safe in Minecraft
■ 100% unofficial!

COMING SOON

Copyright © 2018 by Future Publishing Limited. Minecraft © Microsoft Inc. All Rights Reserved.